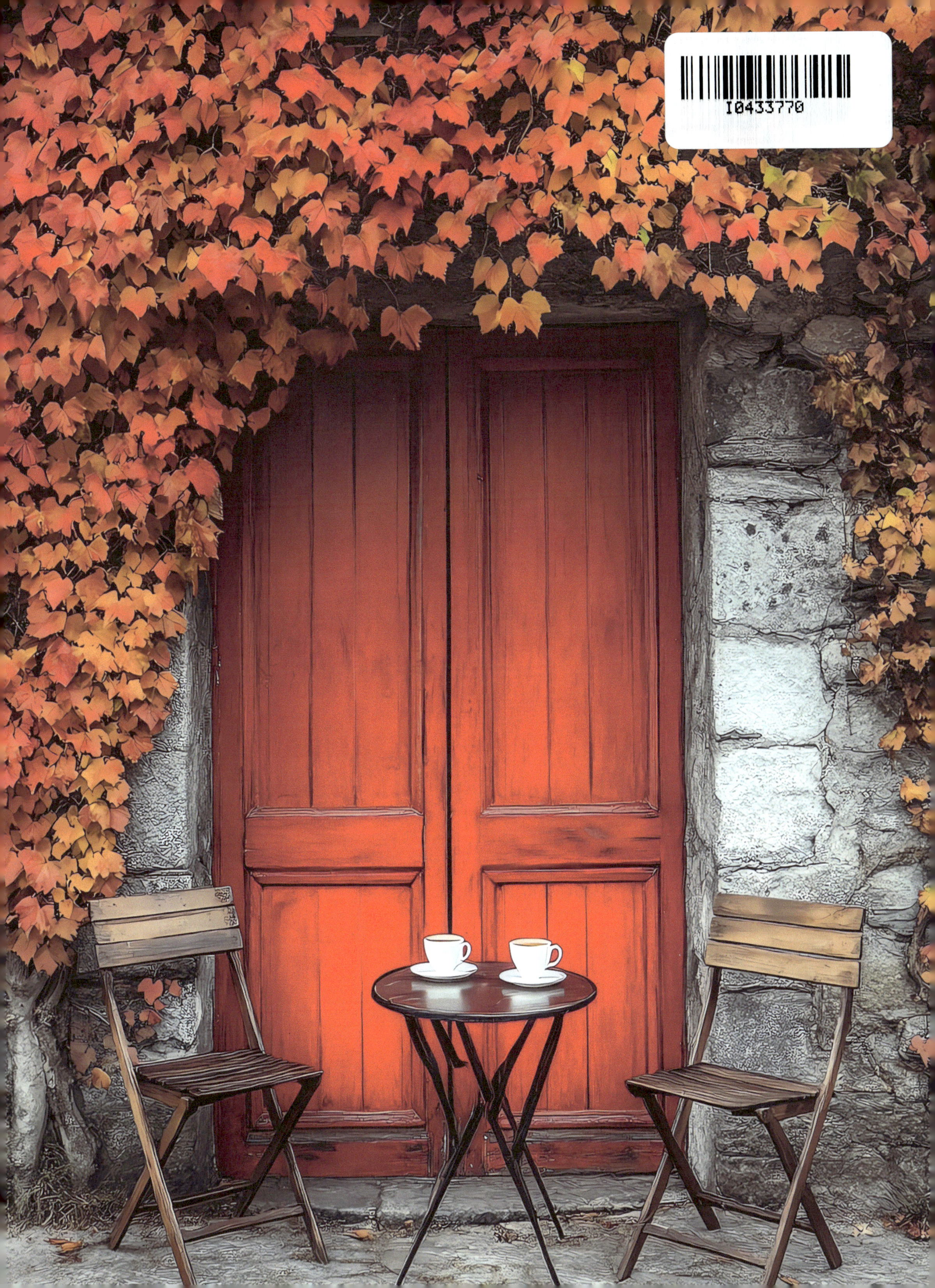

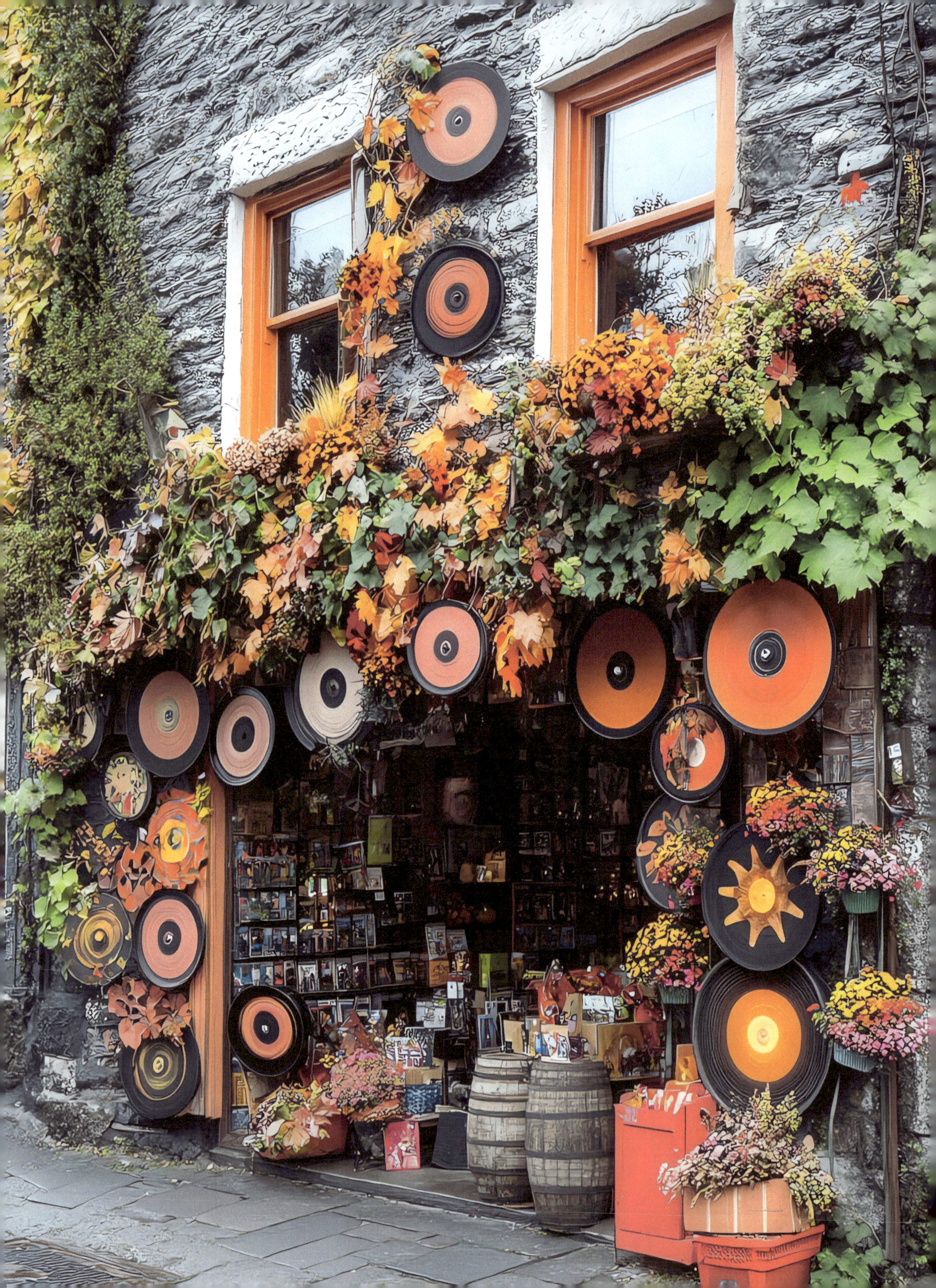

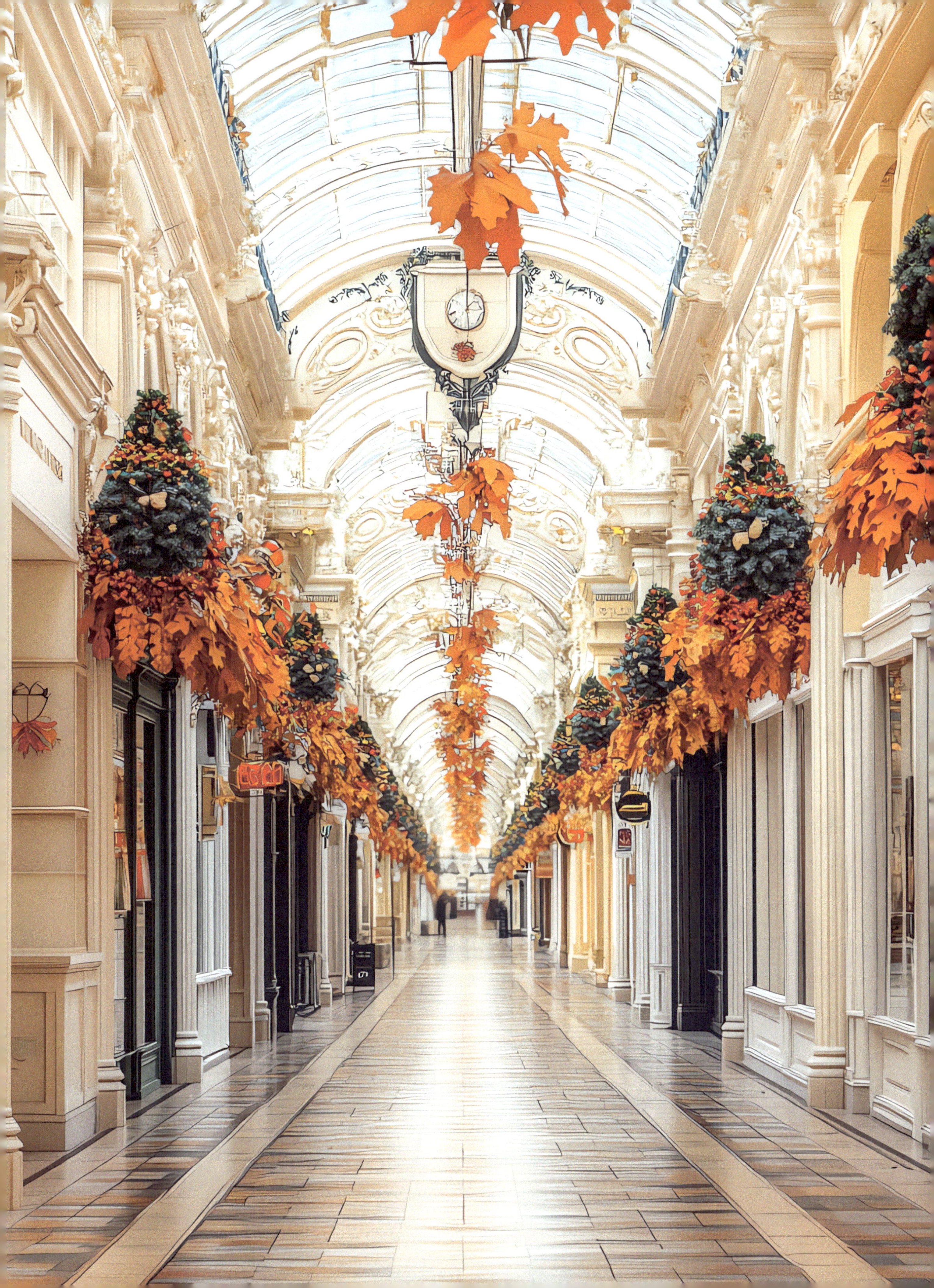

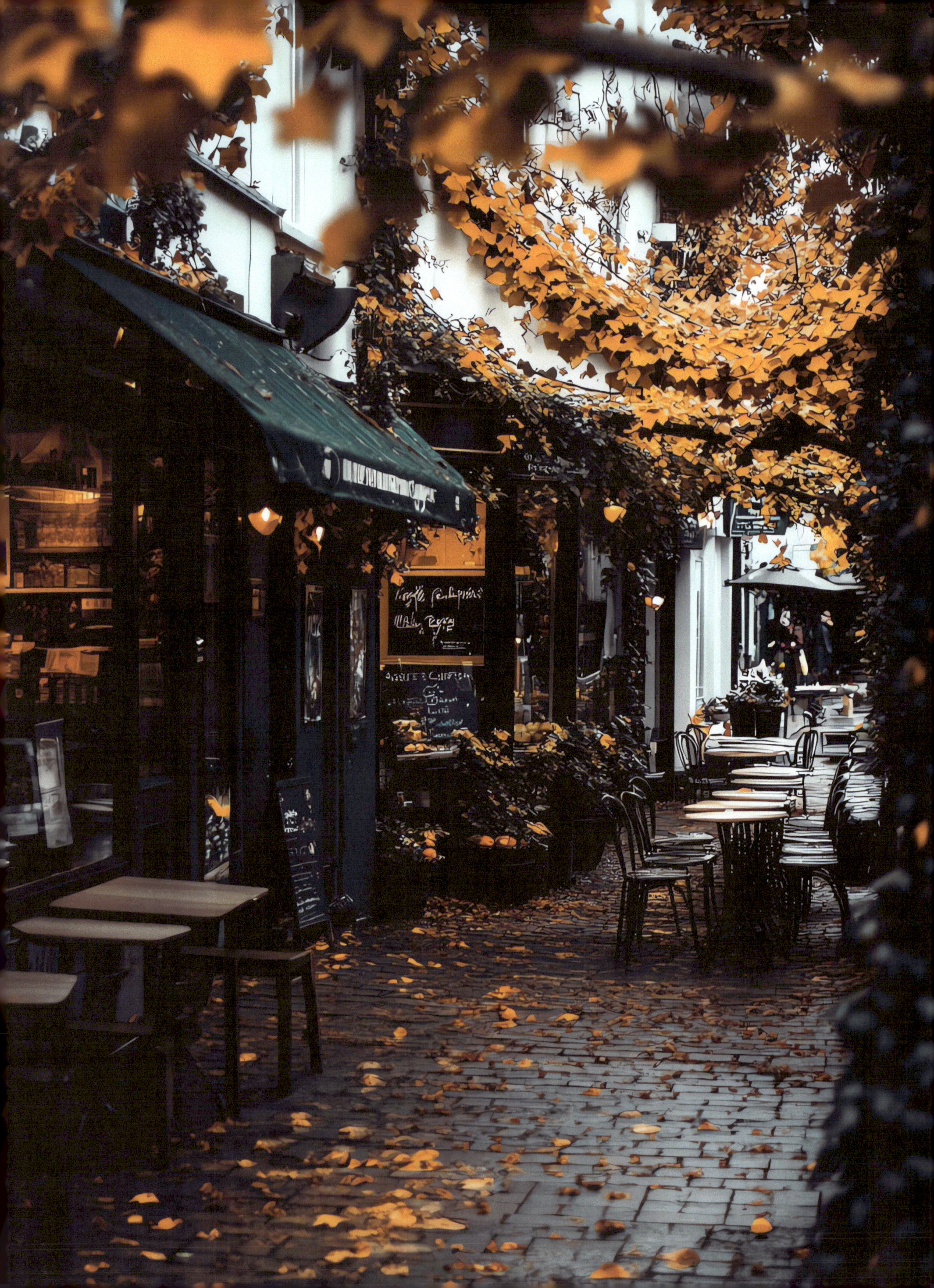

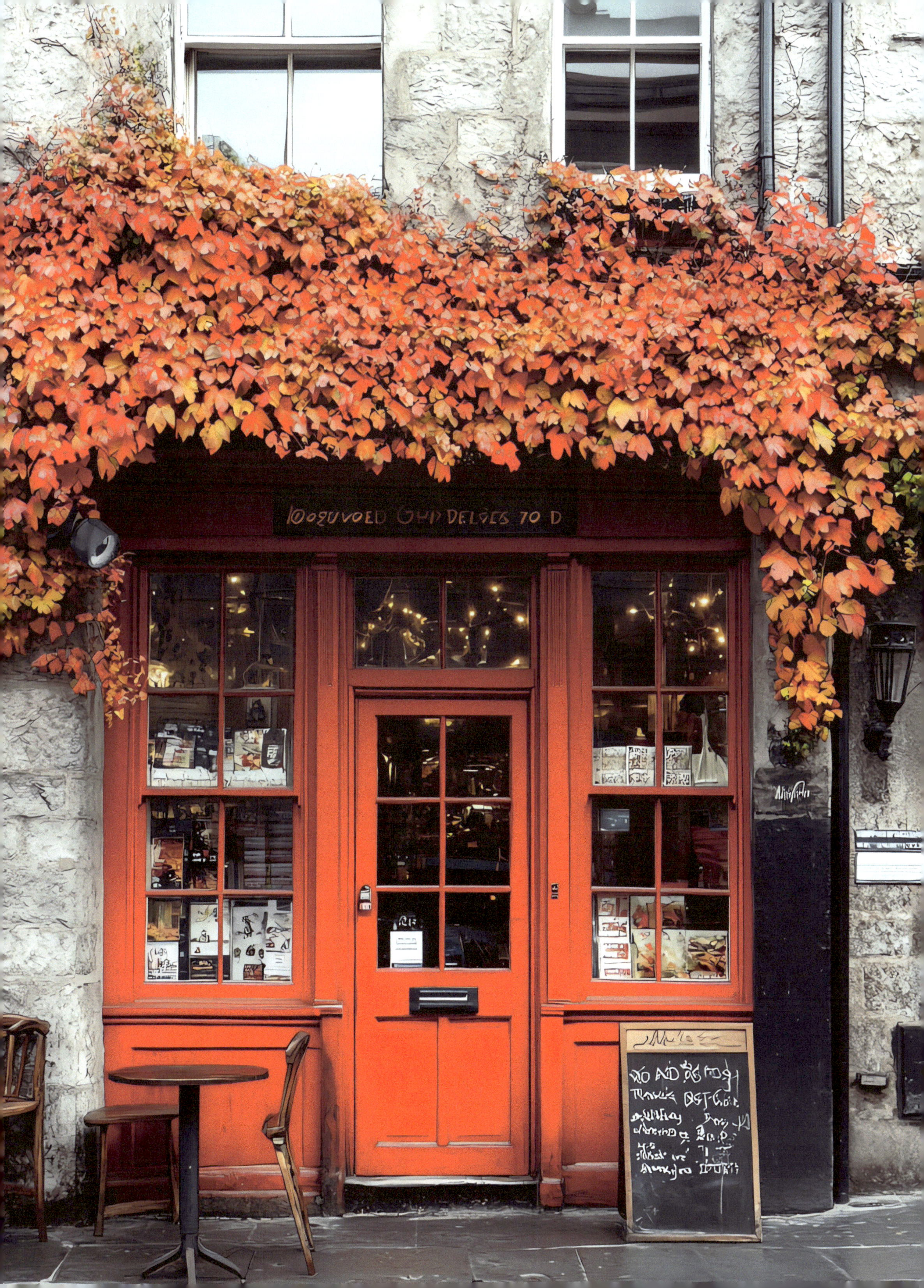

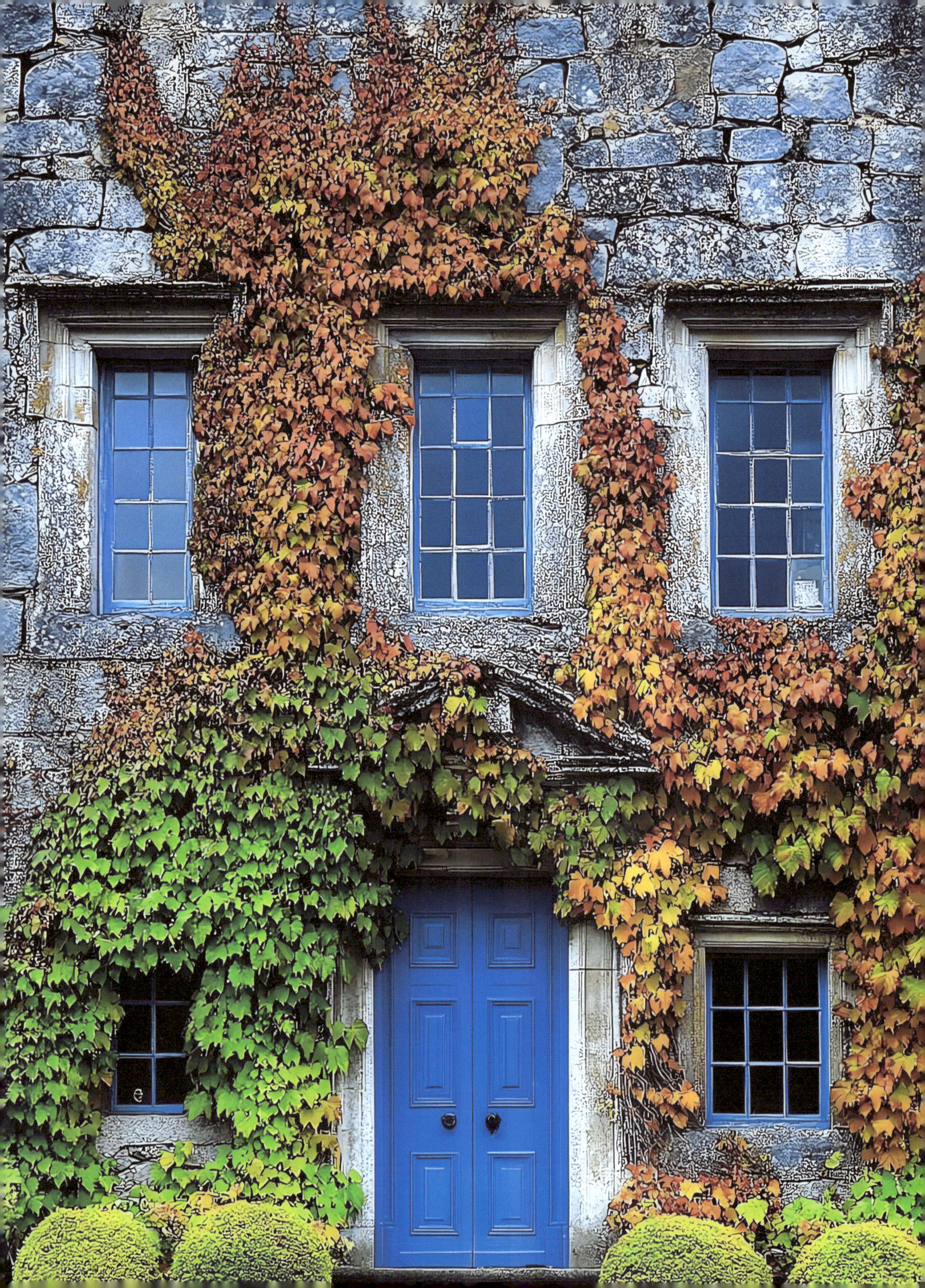

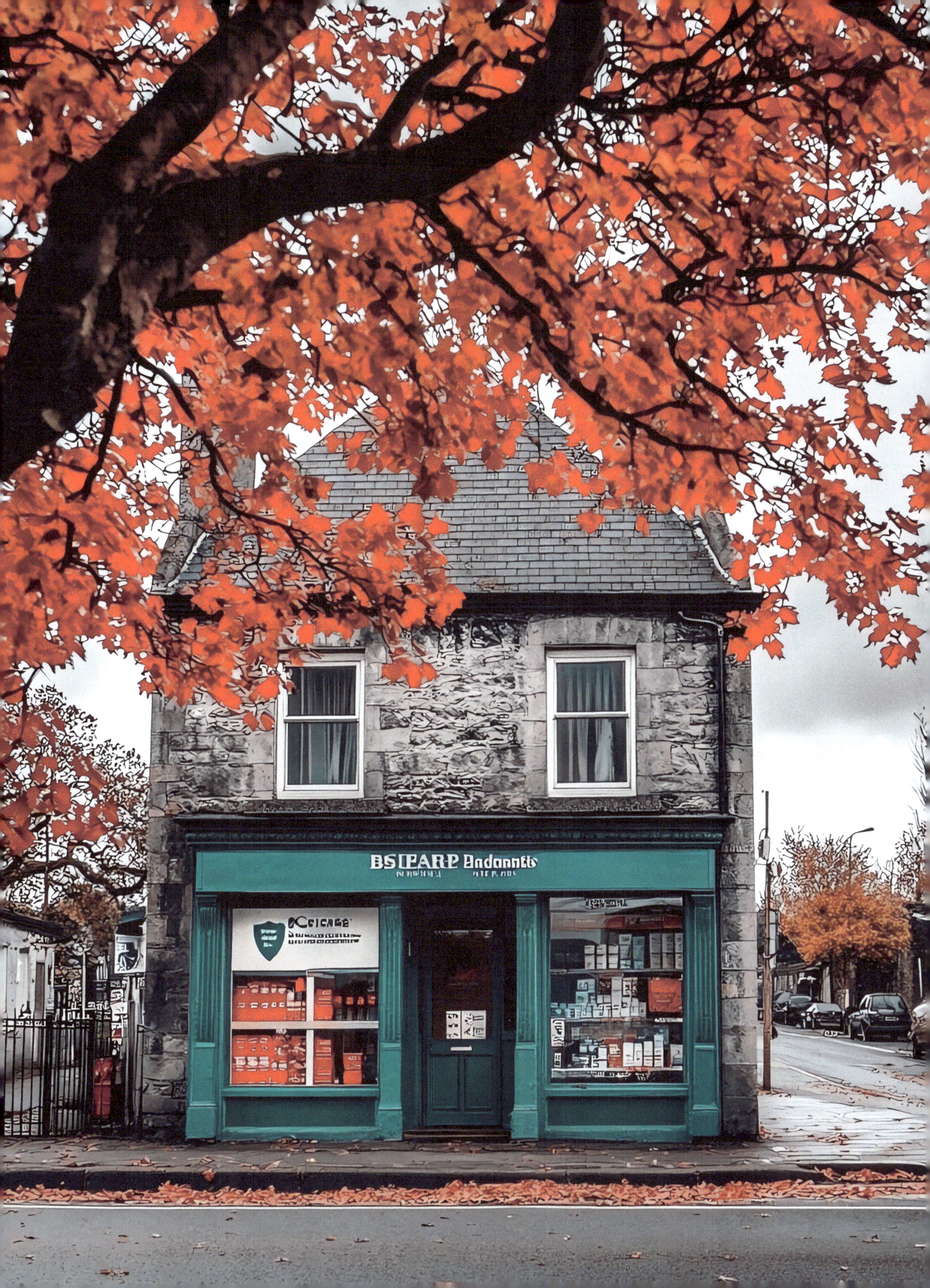

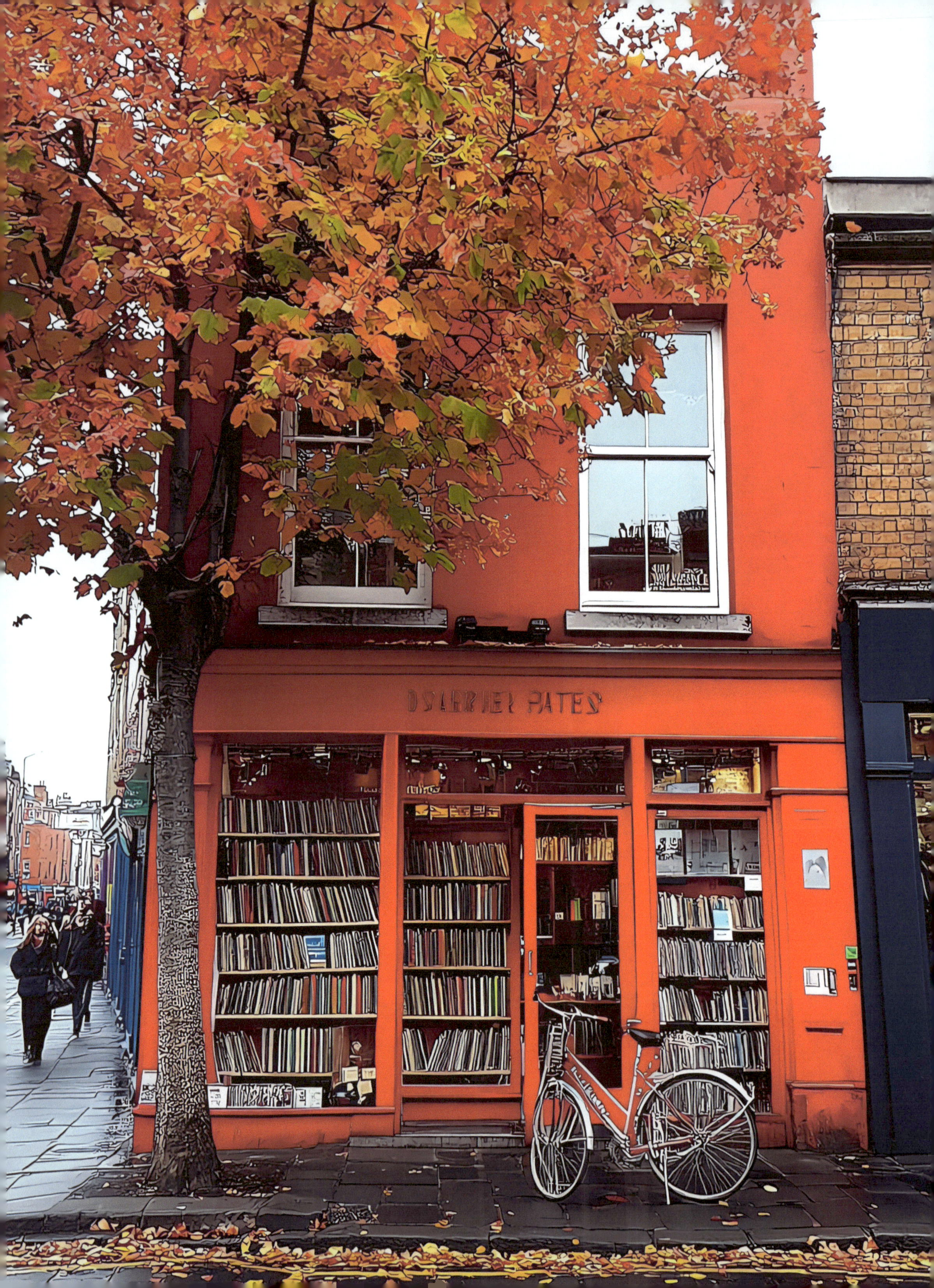

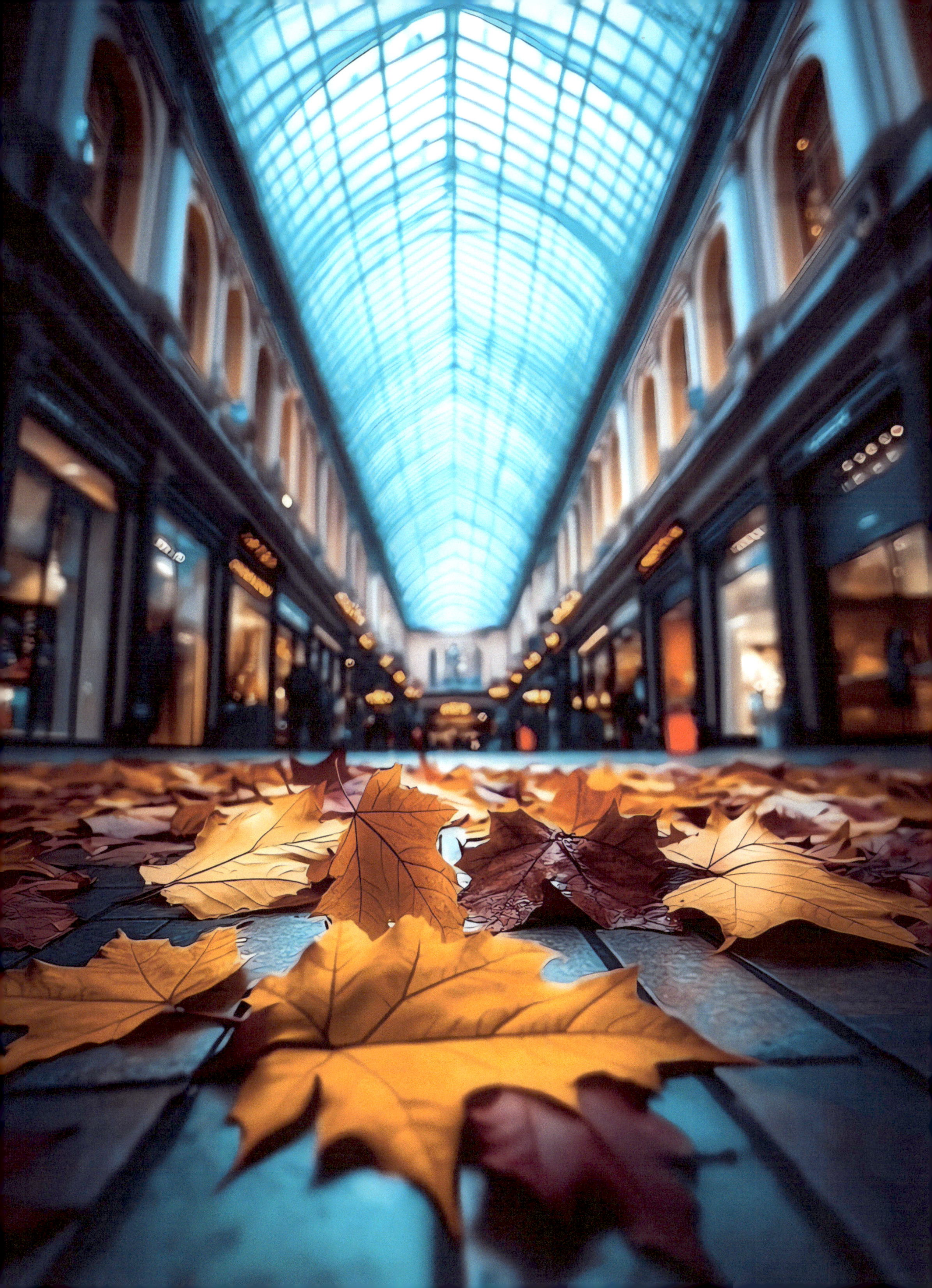

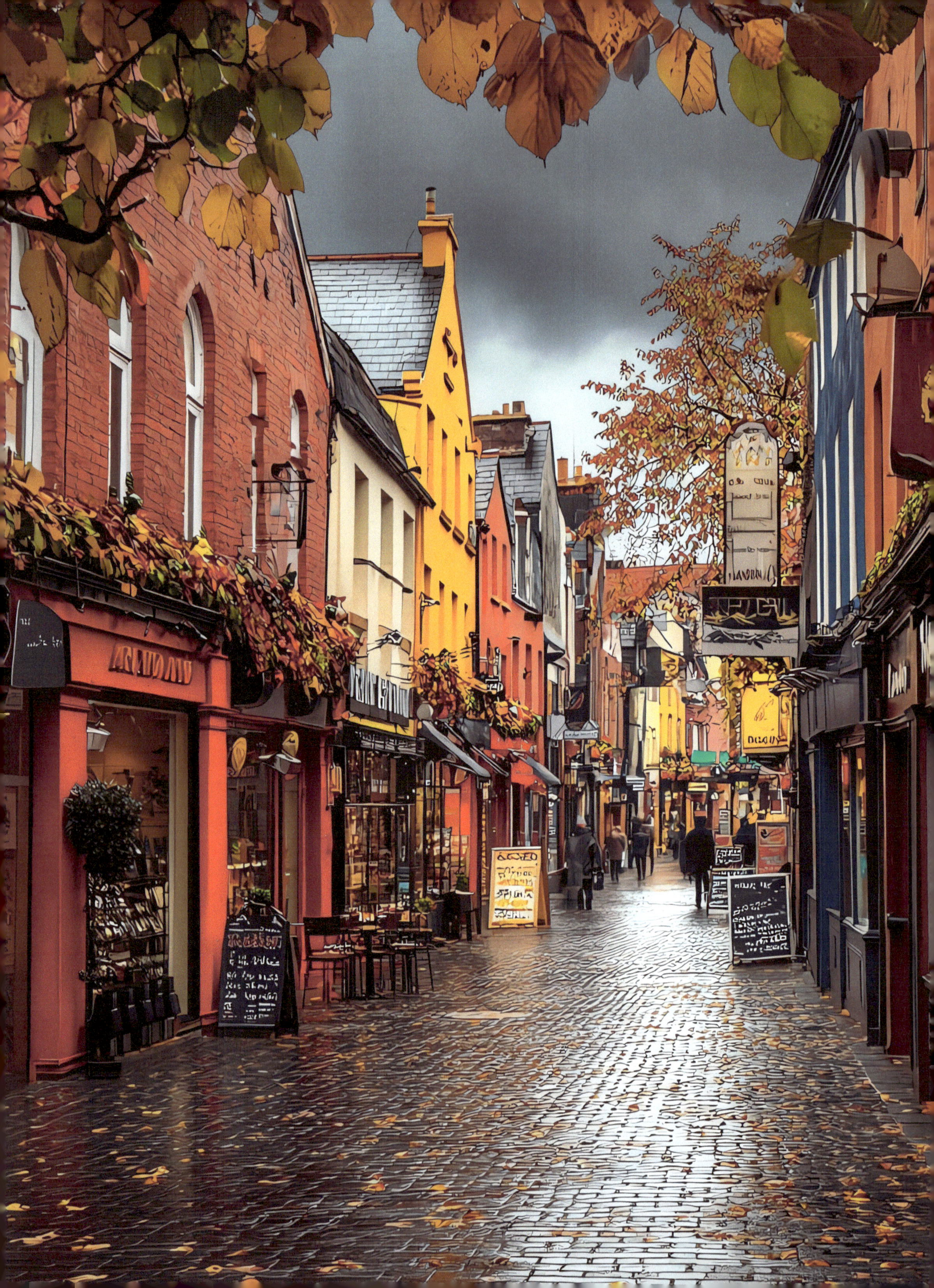

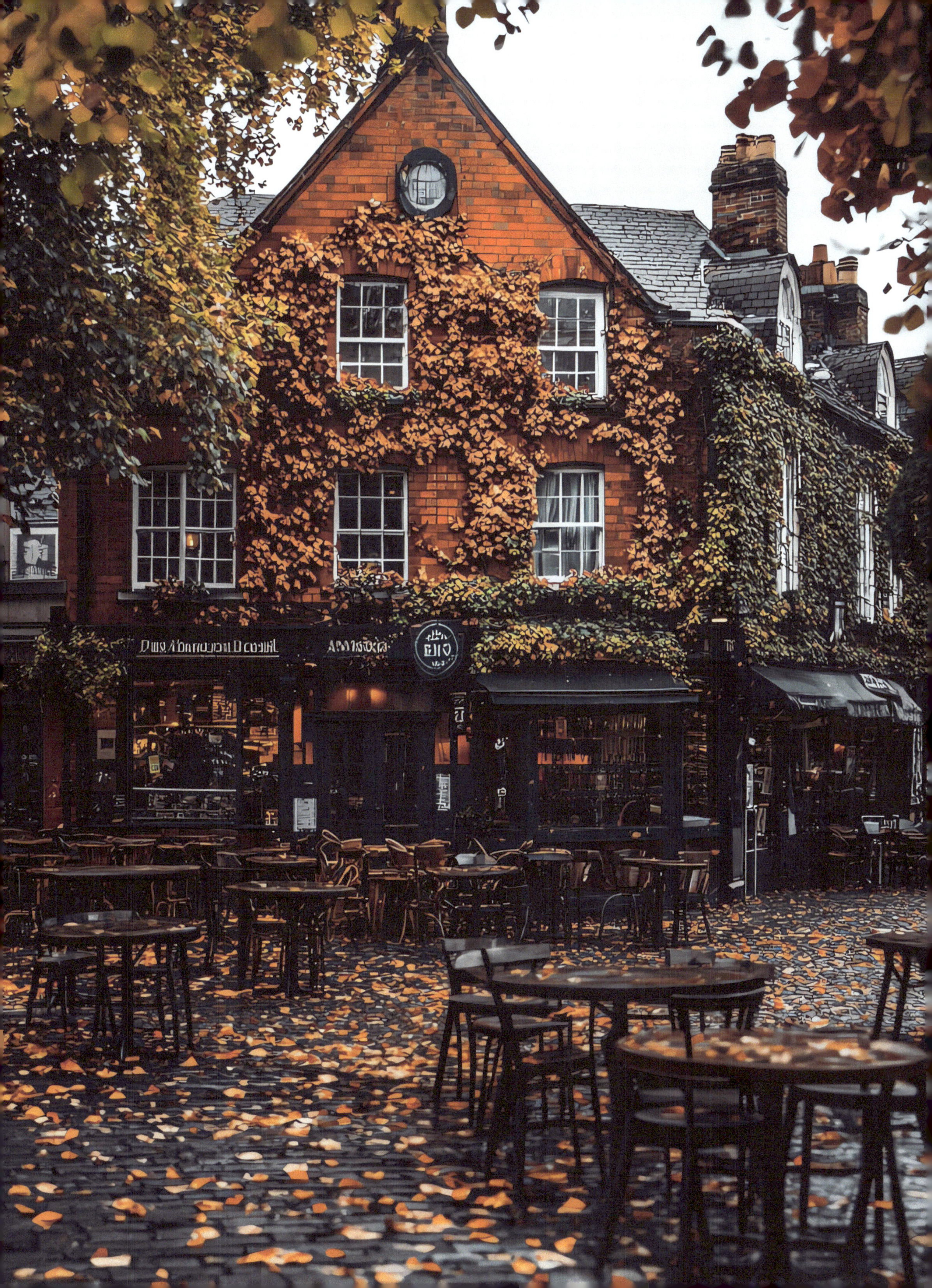

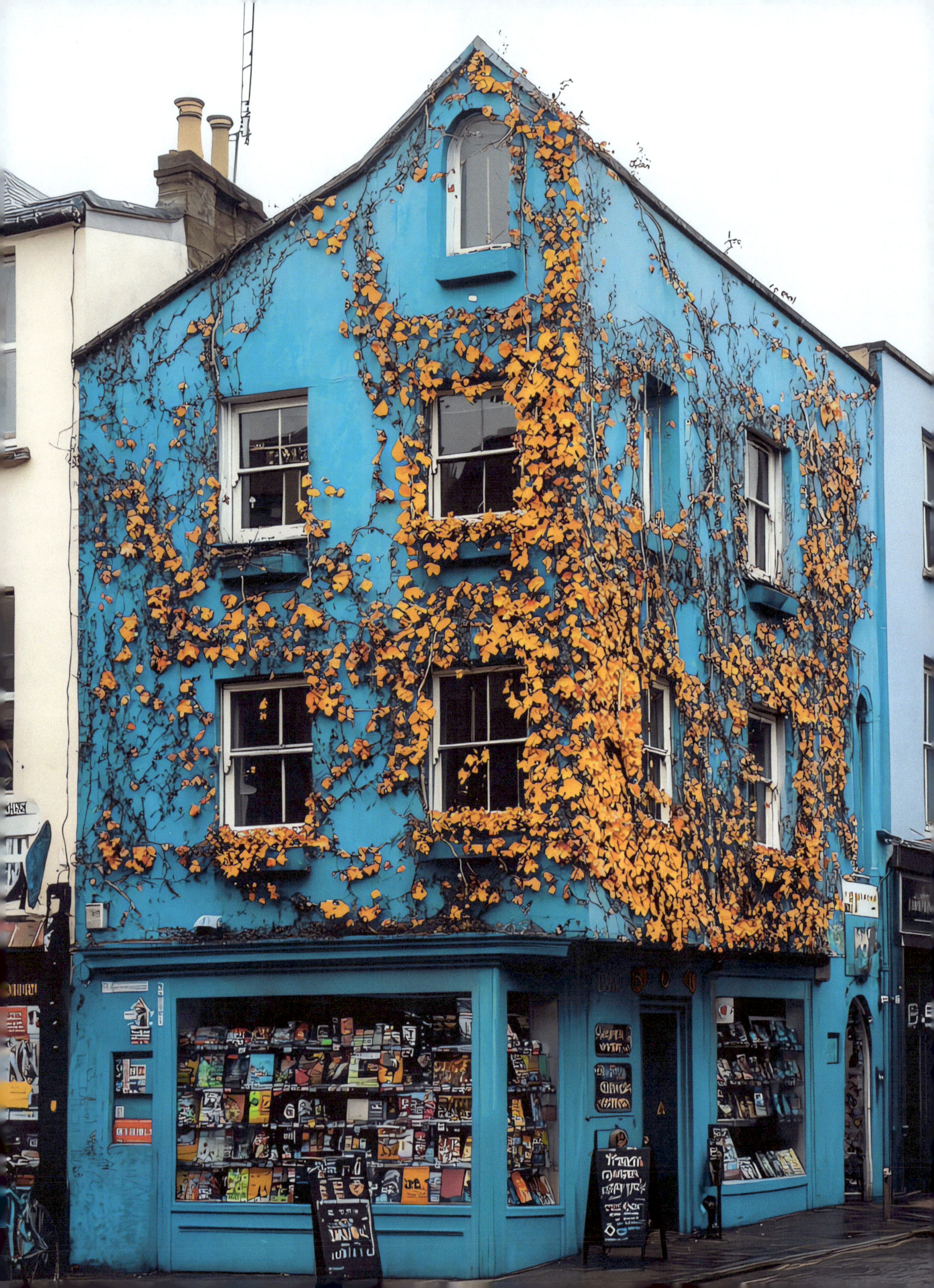

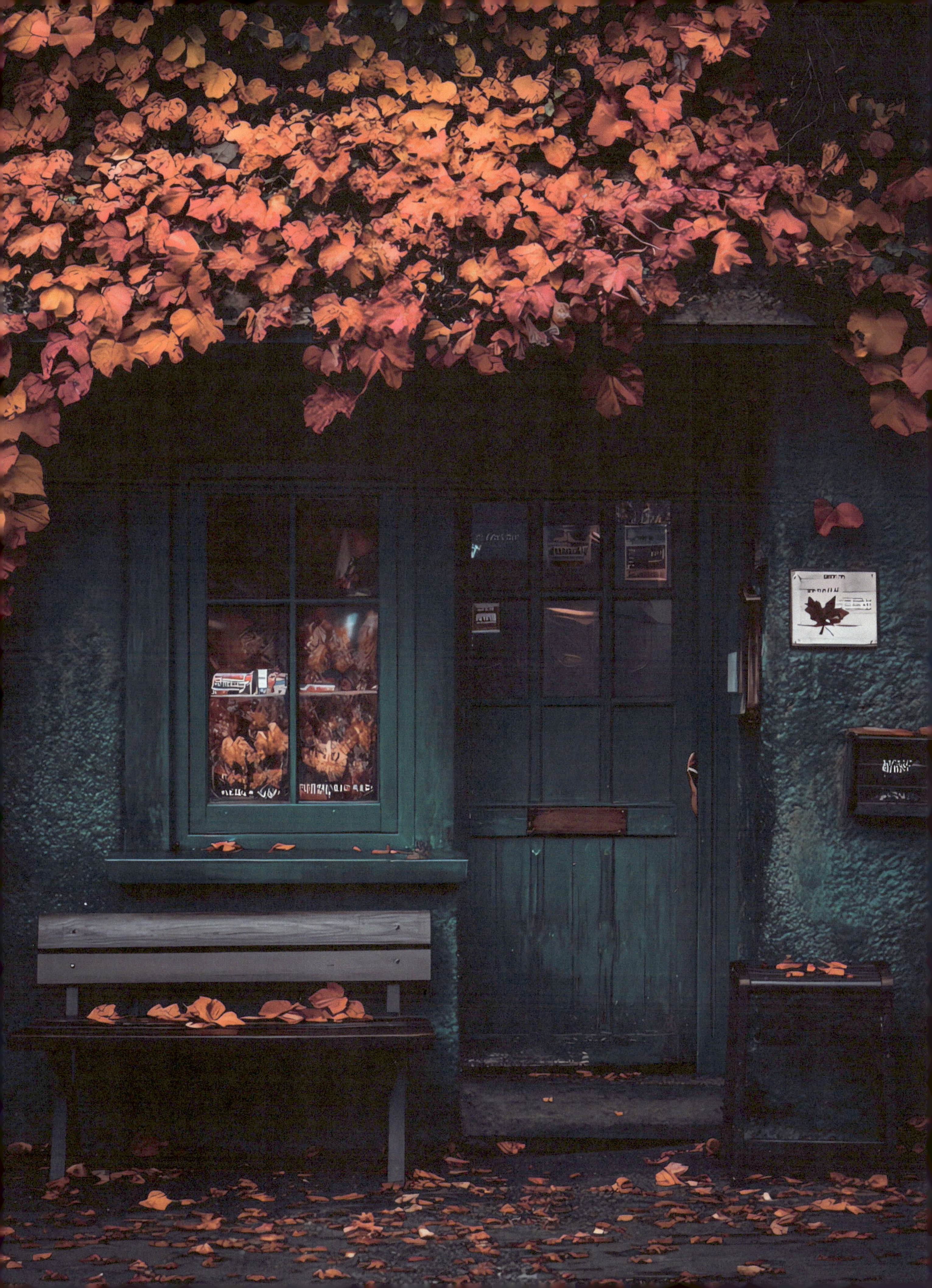

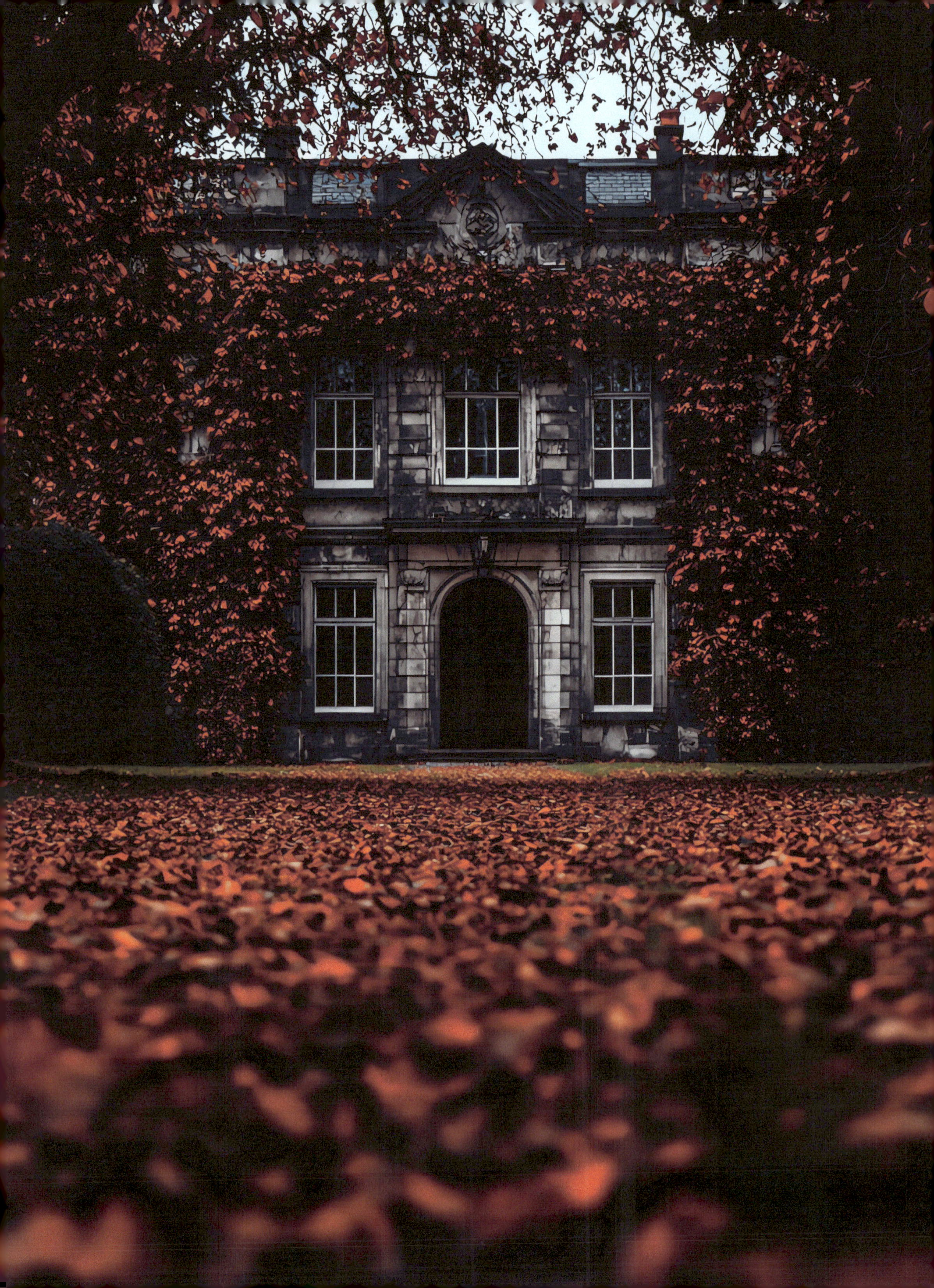

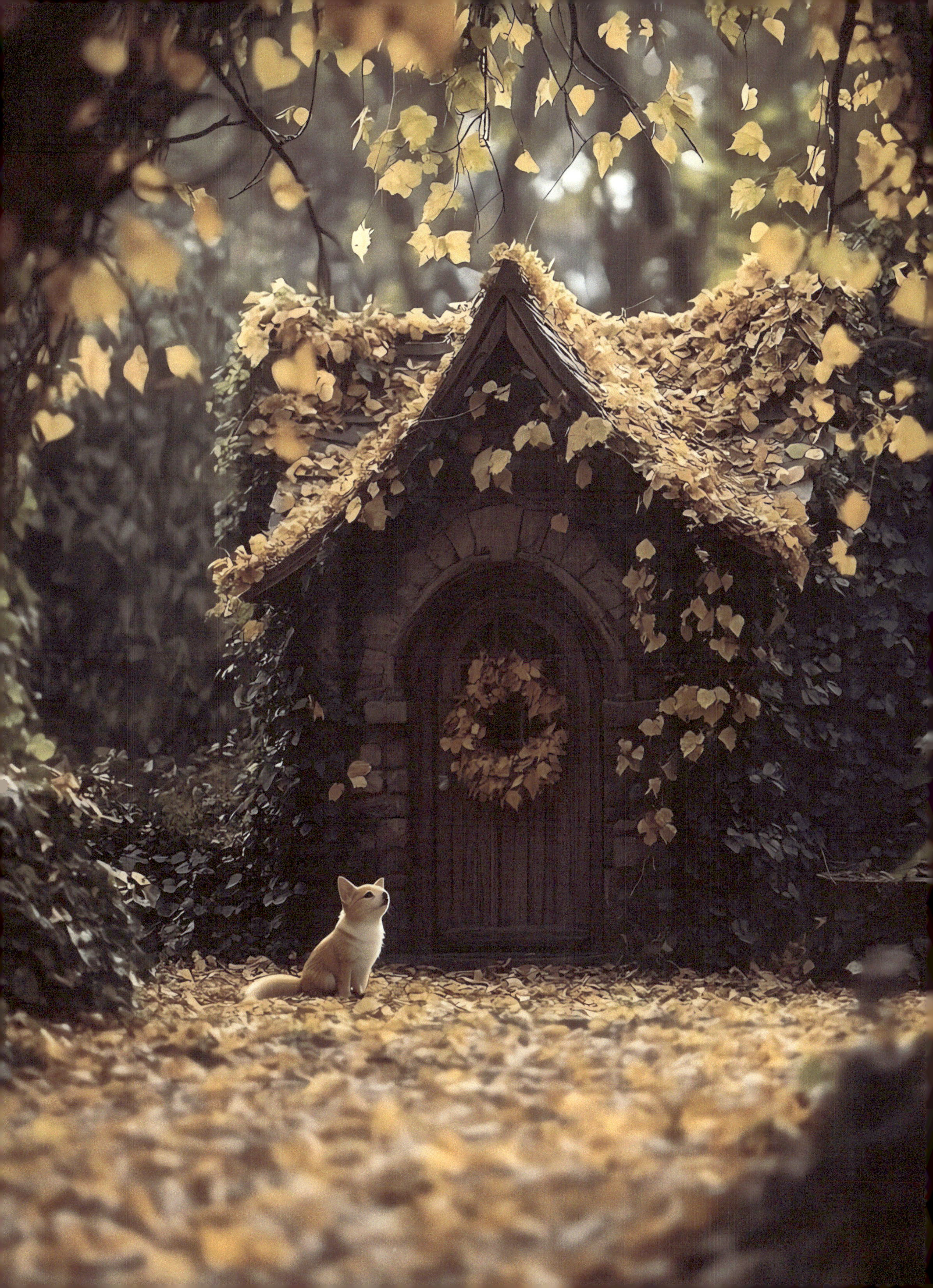

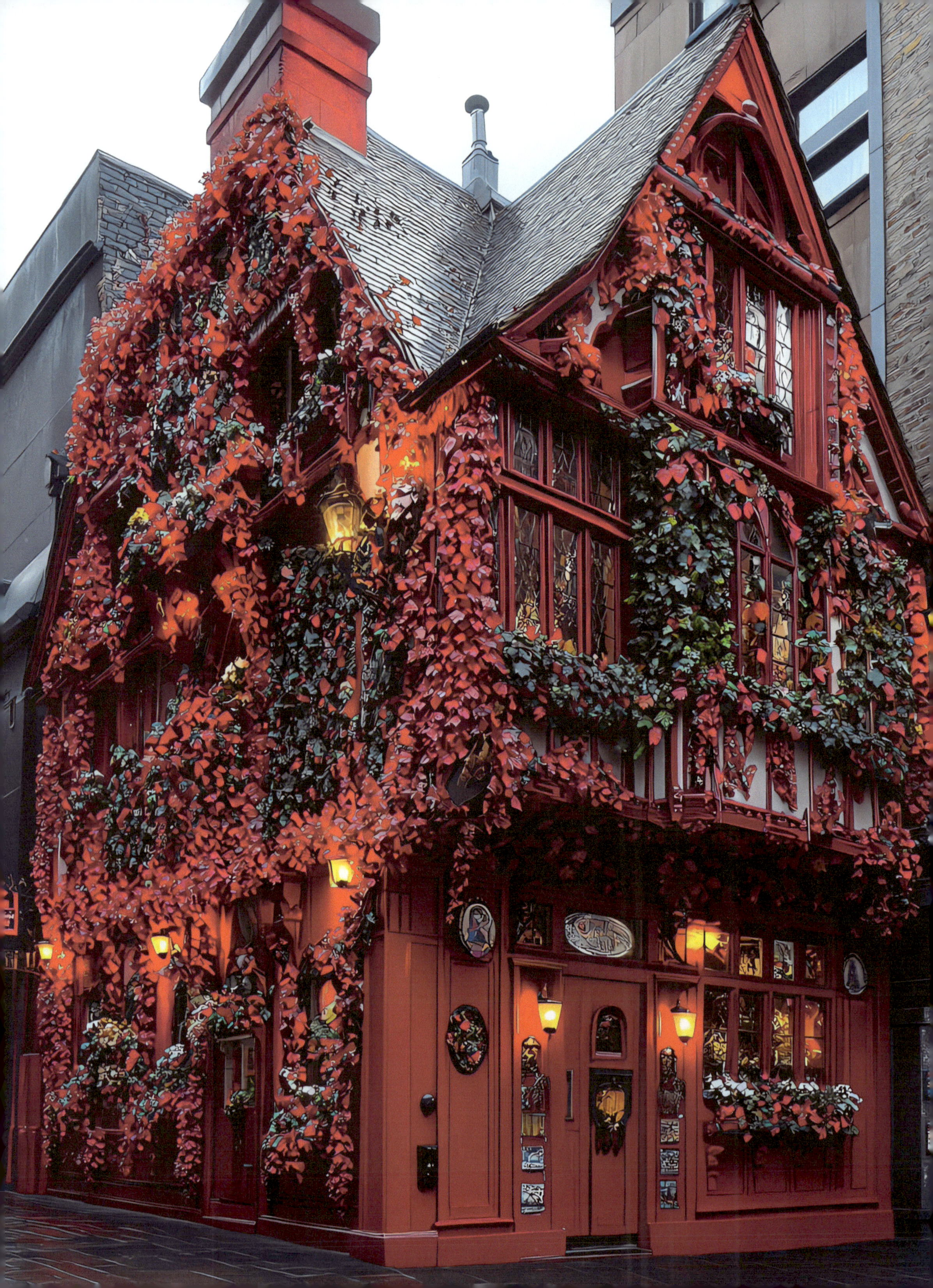

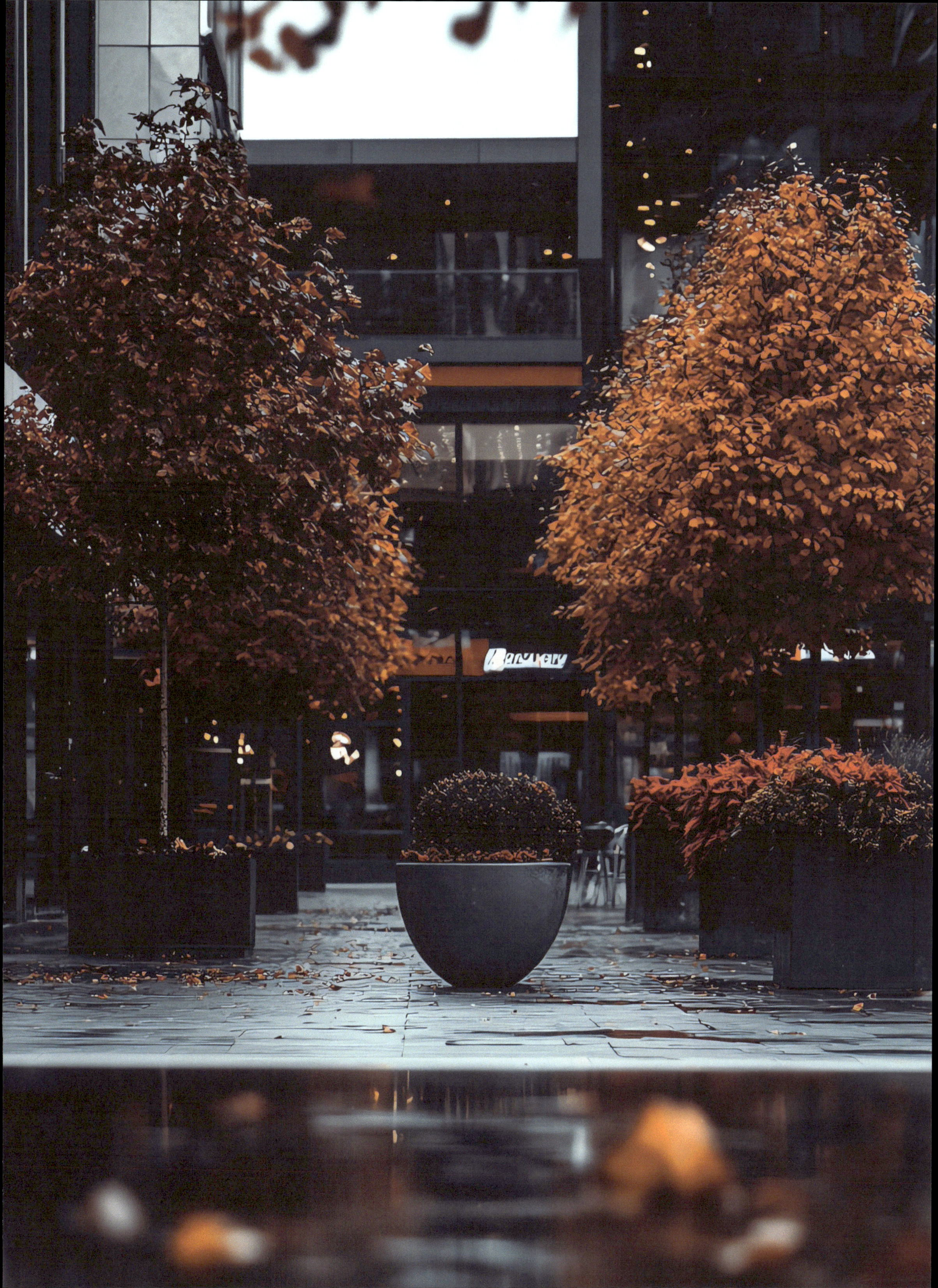

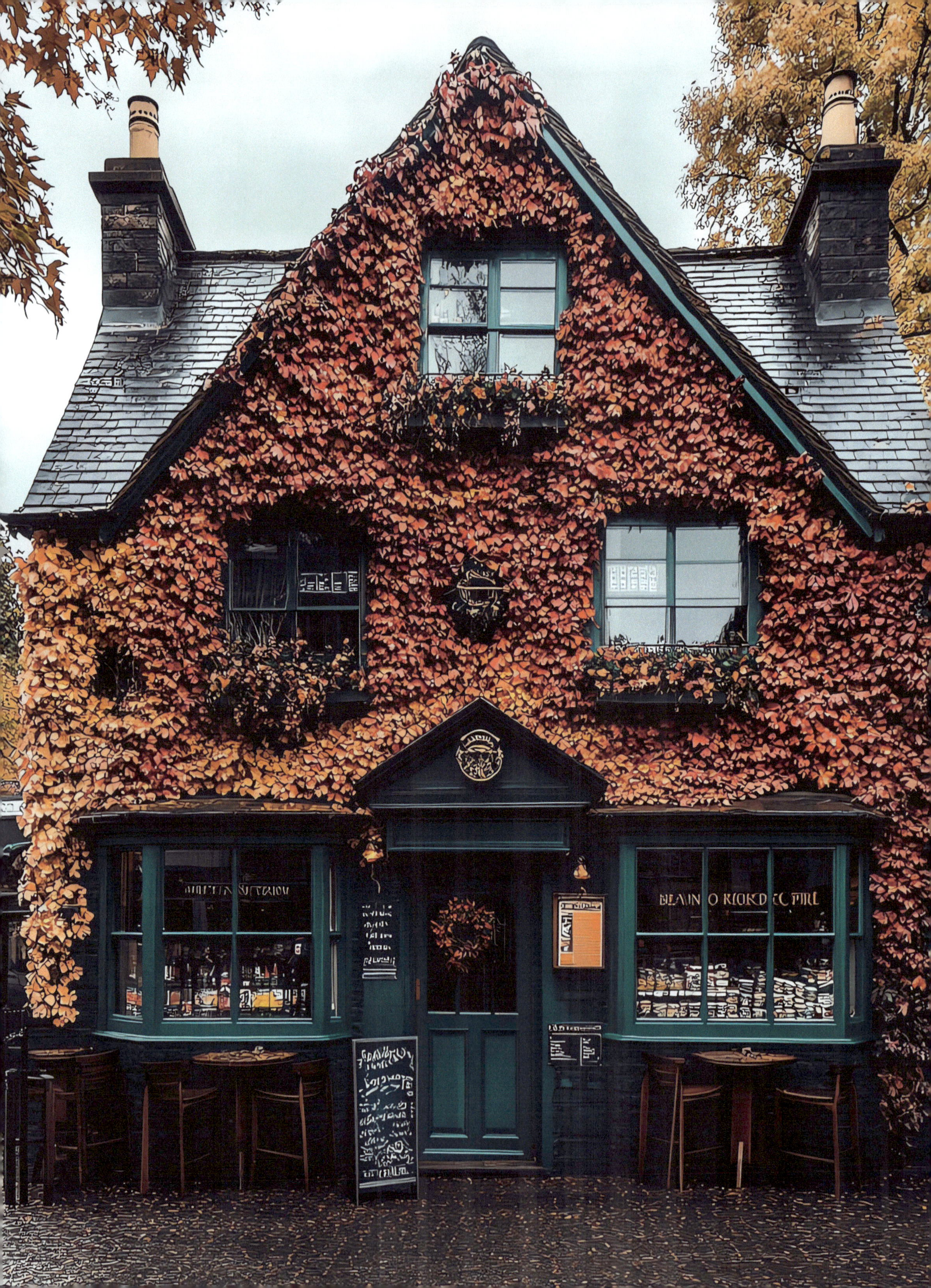

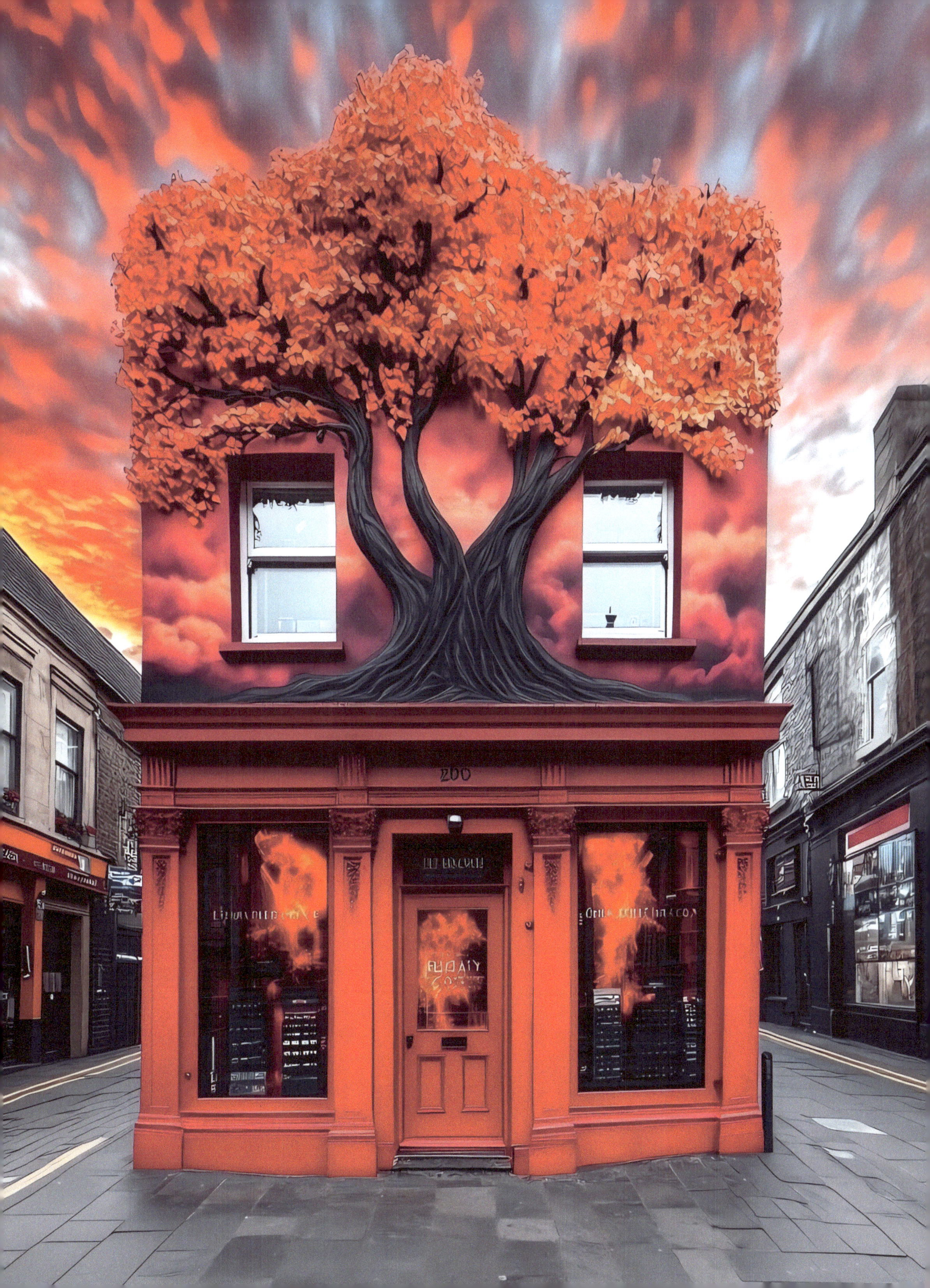

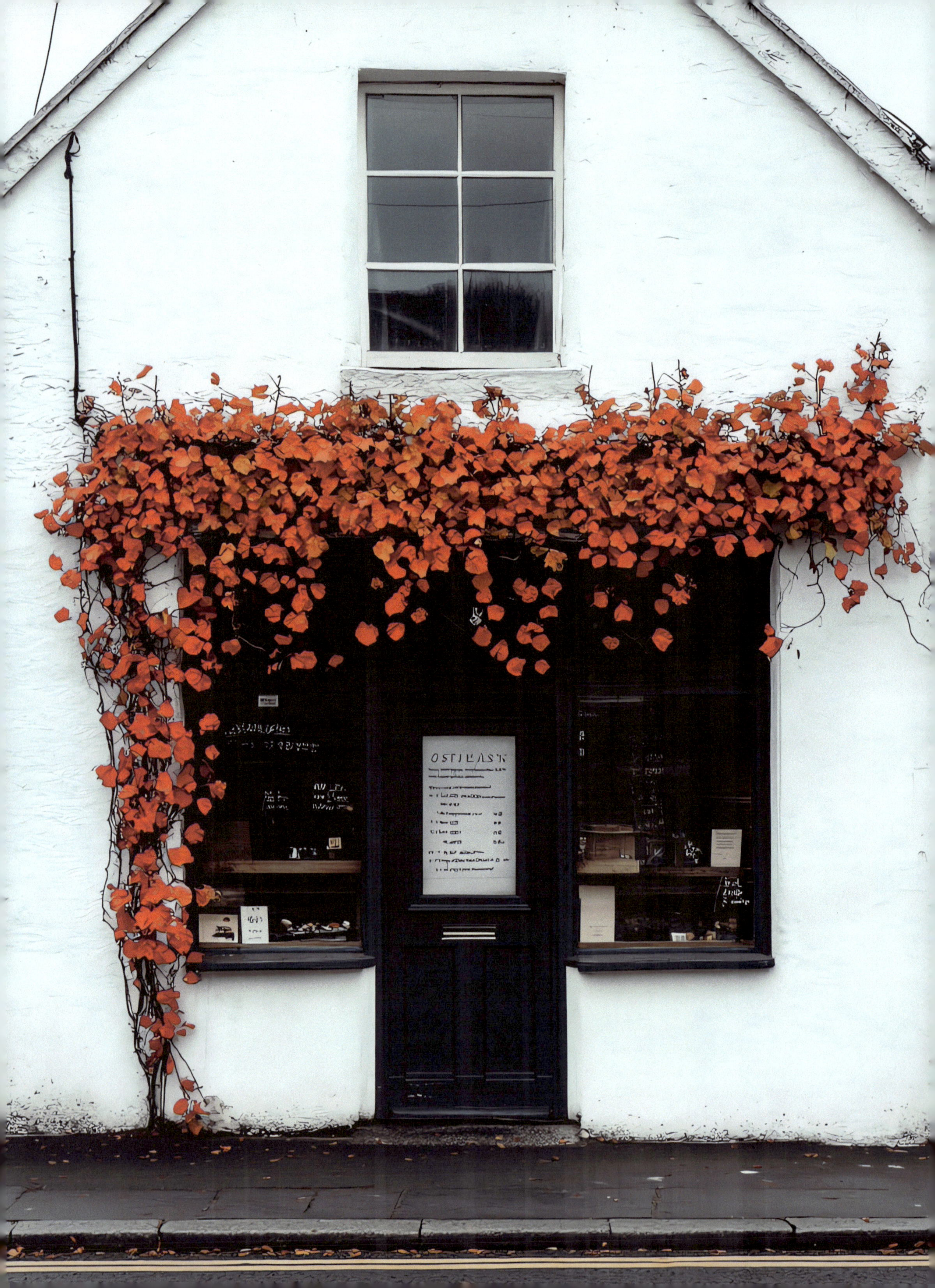

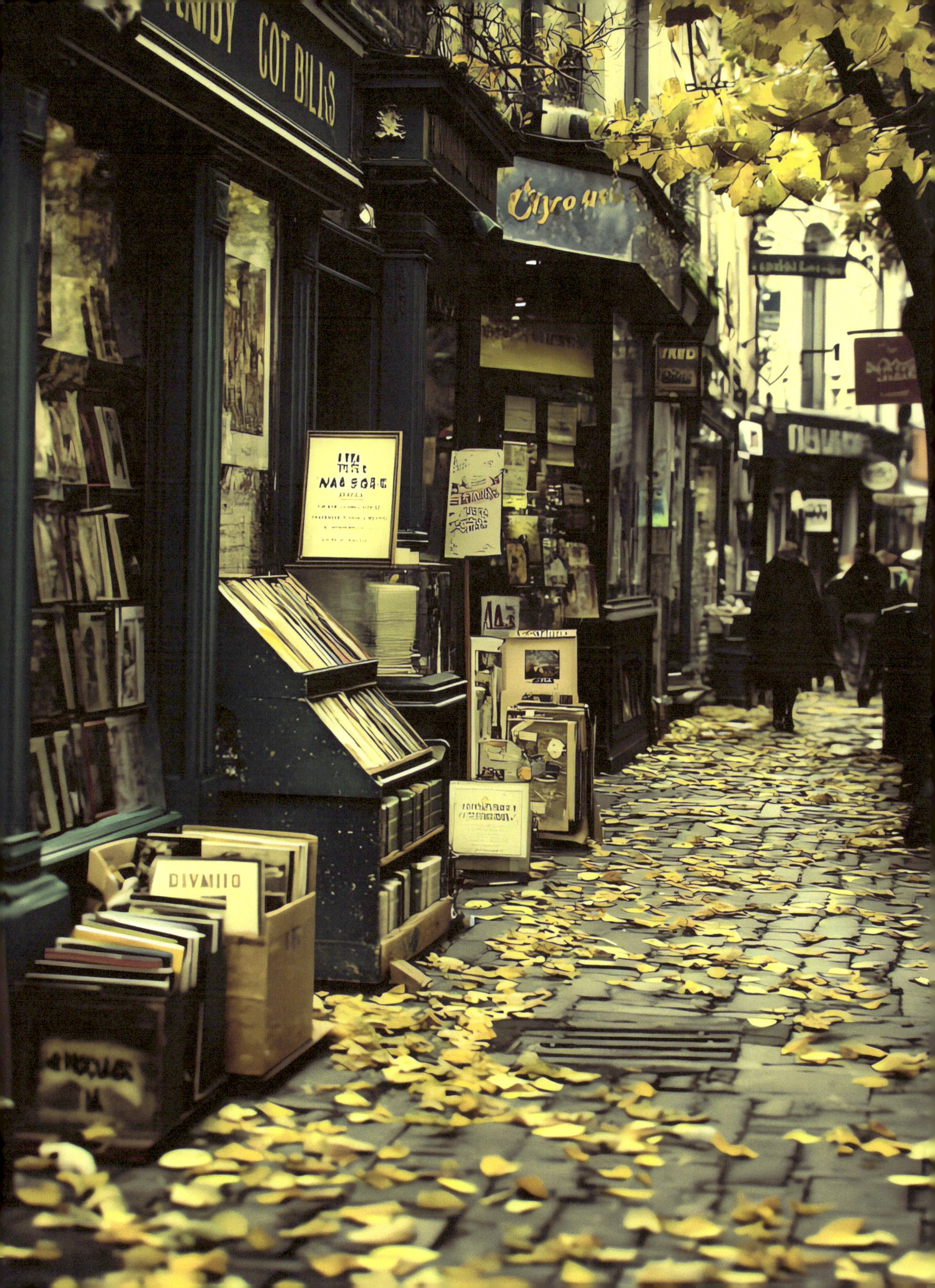

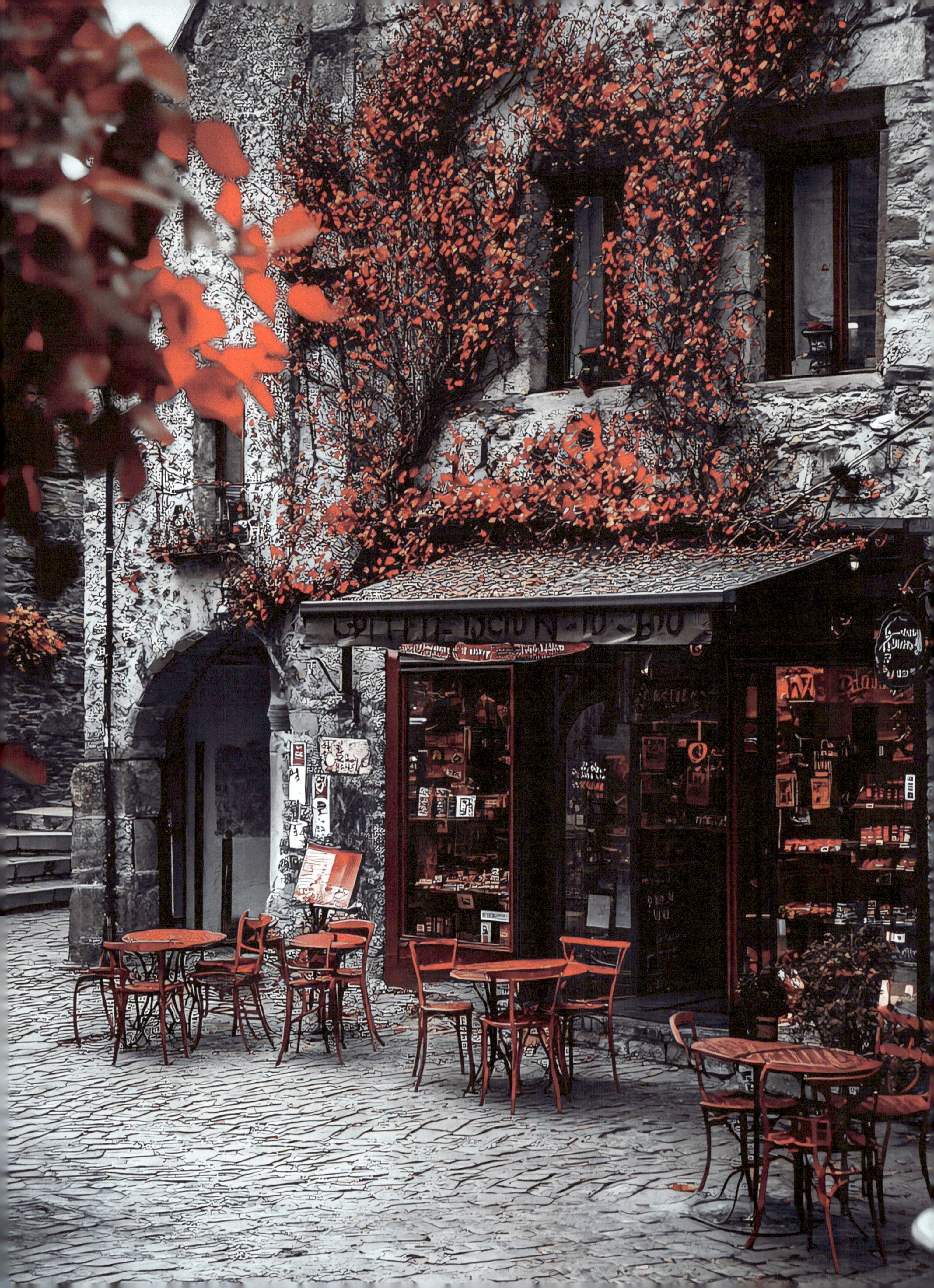

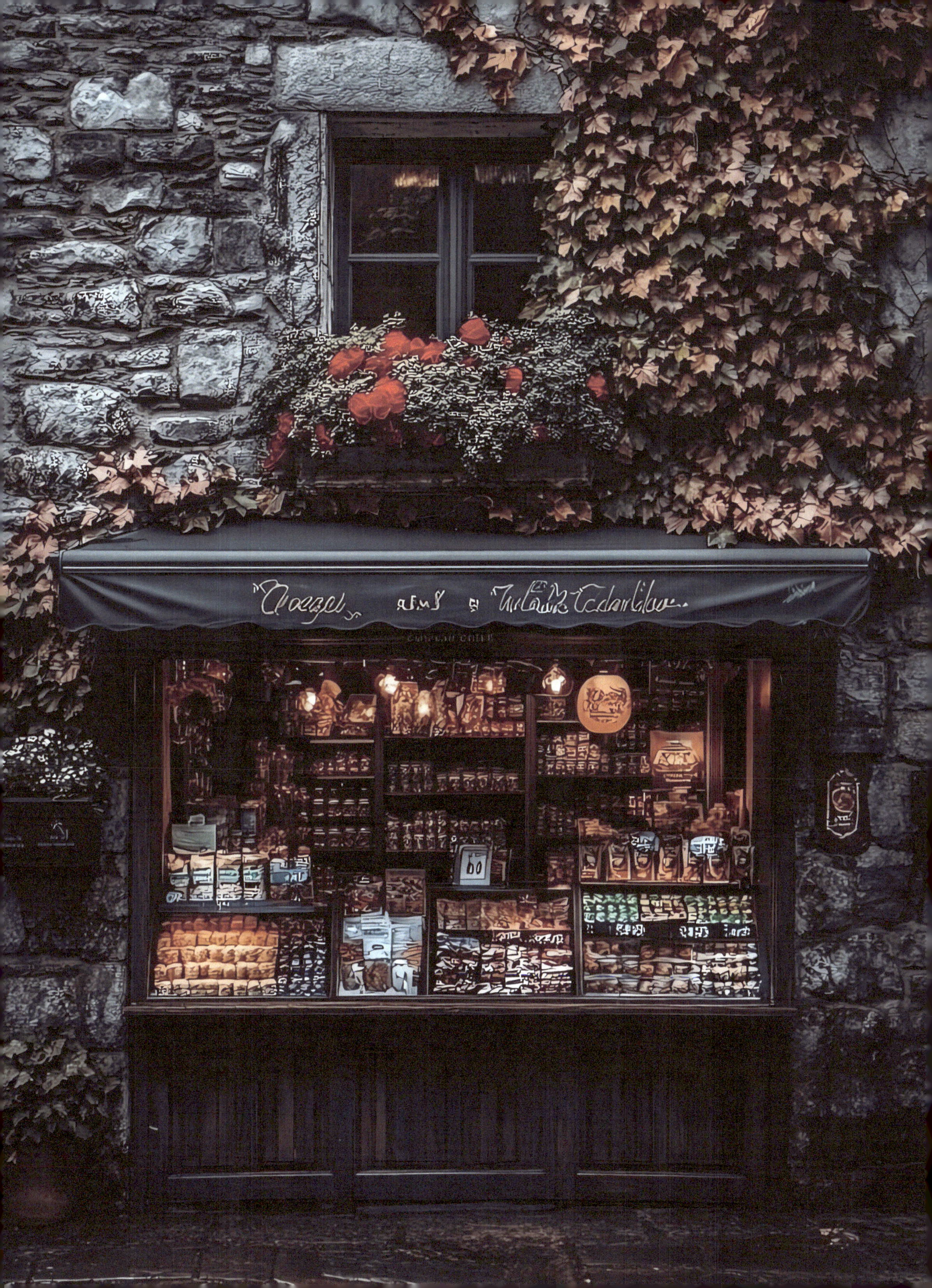

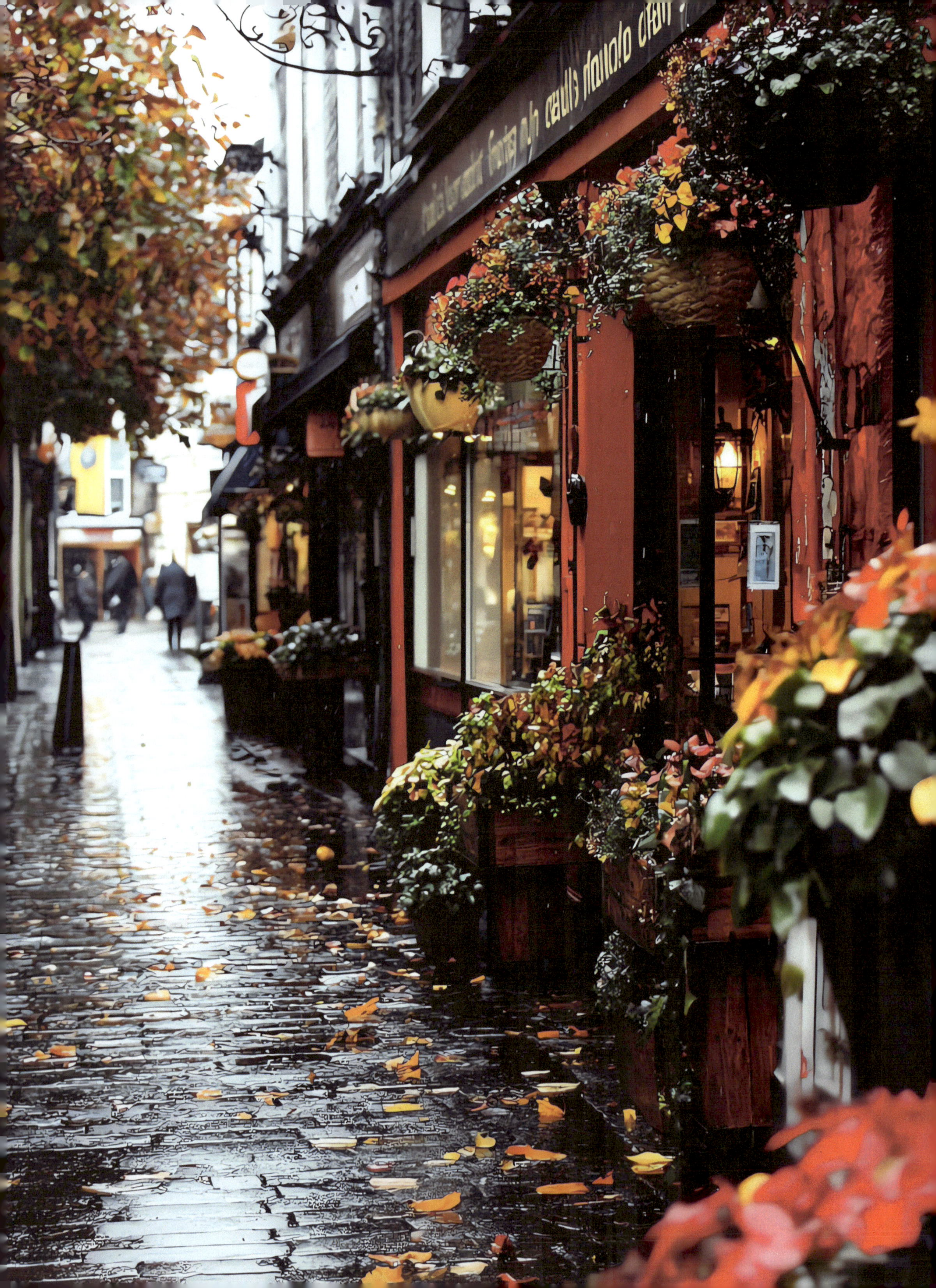

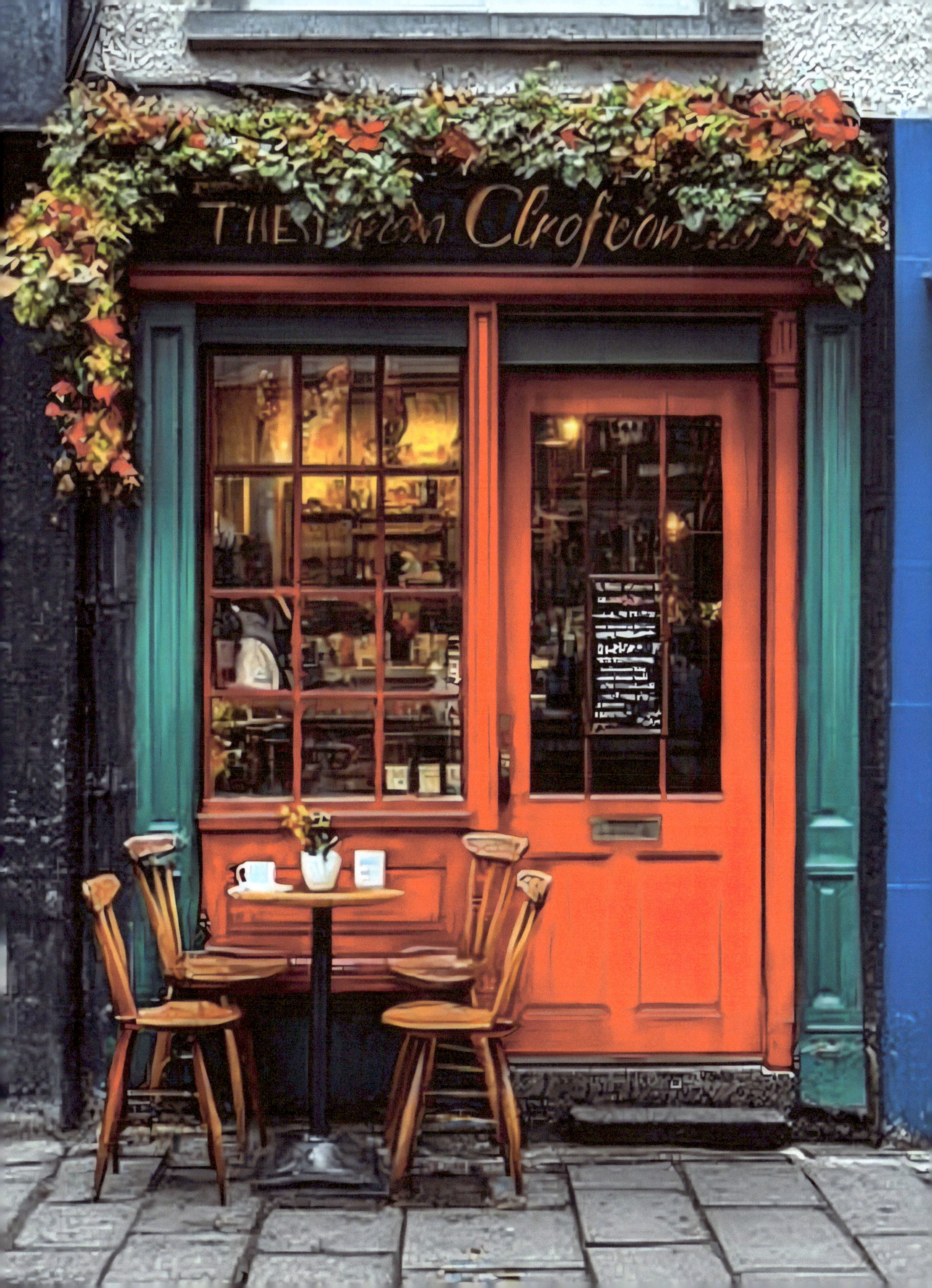

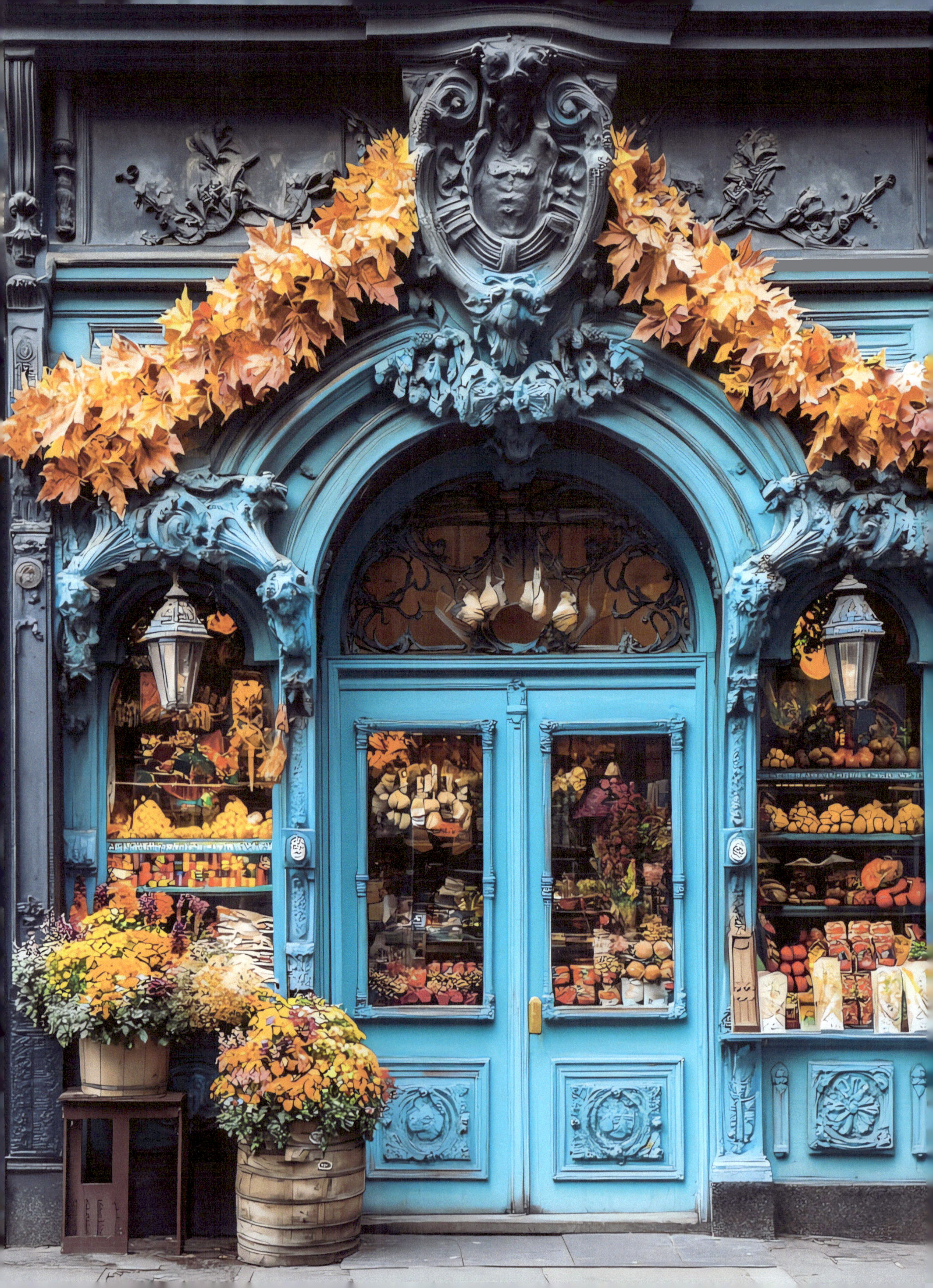

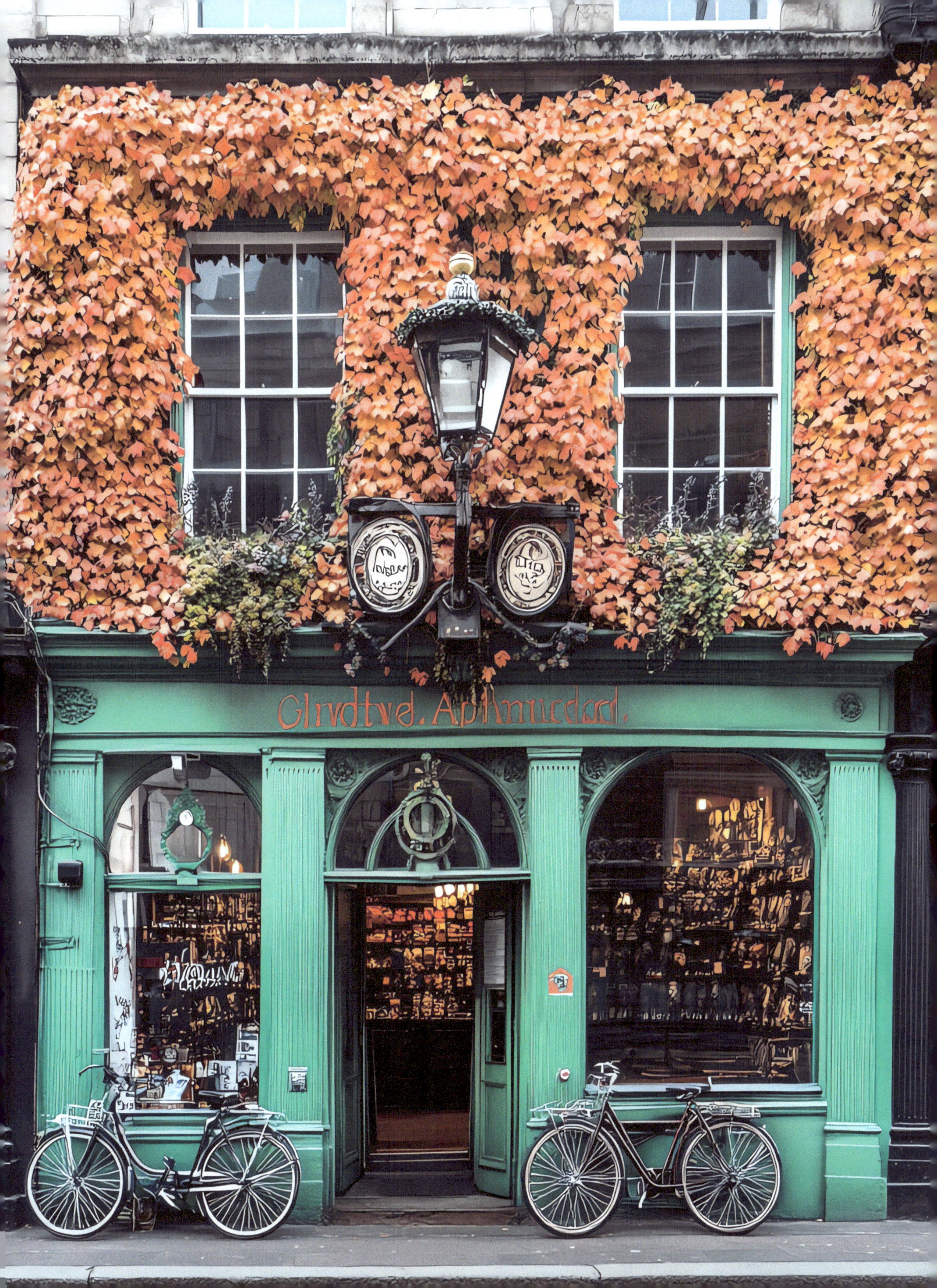

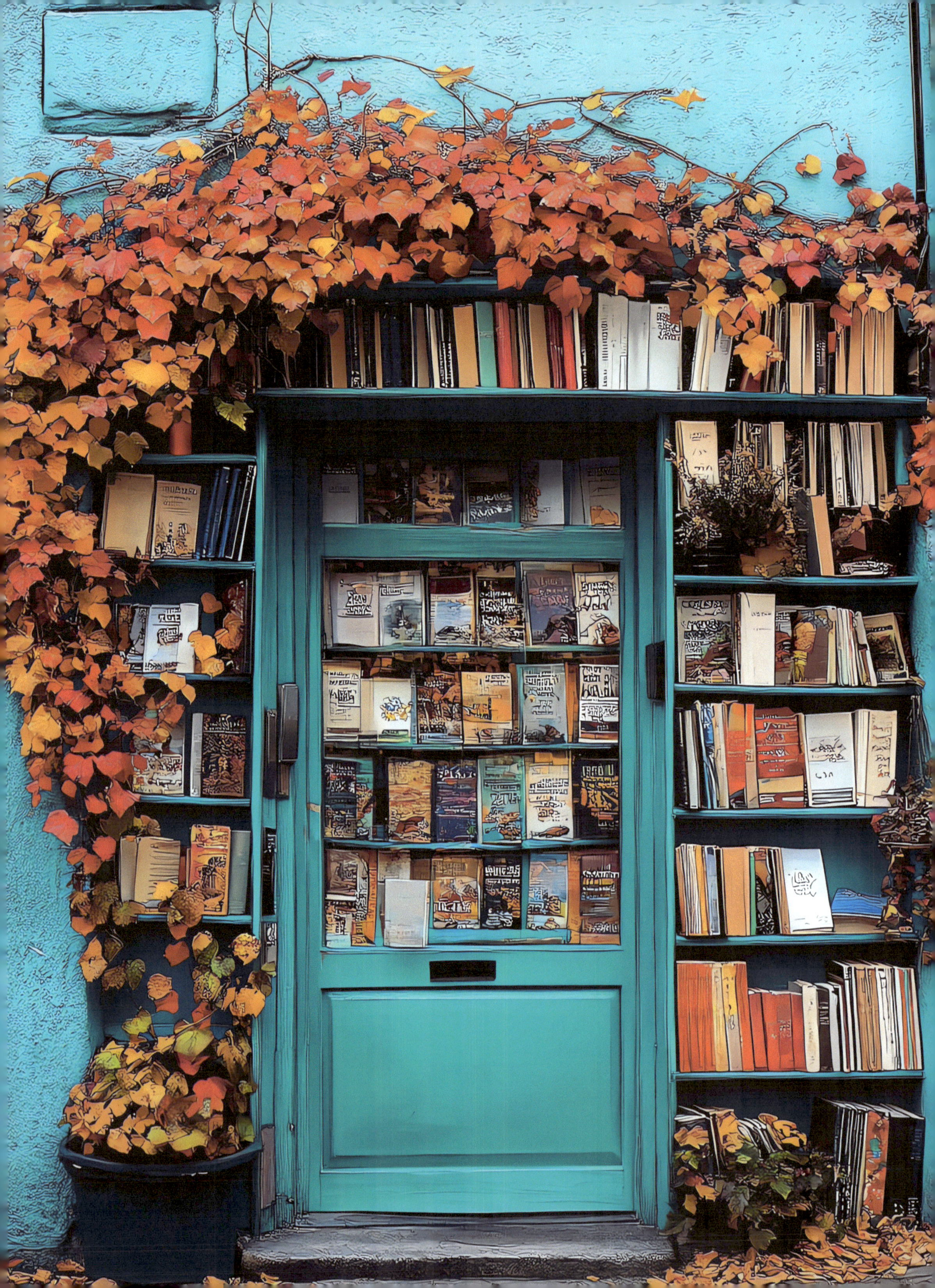

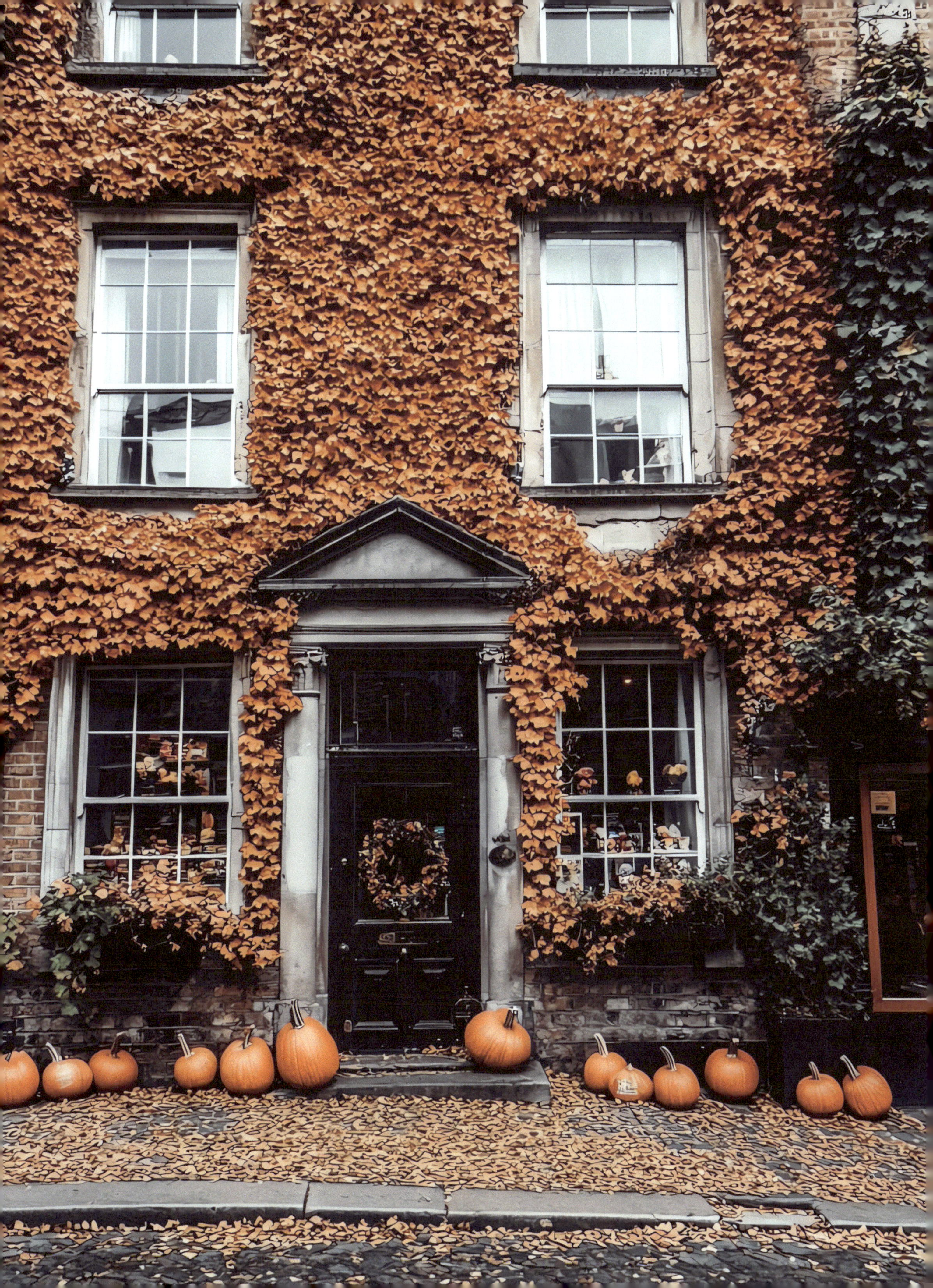

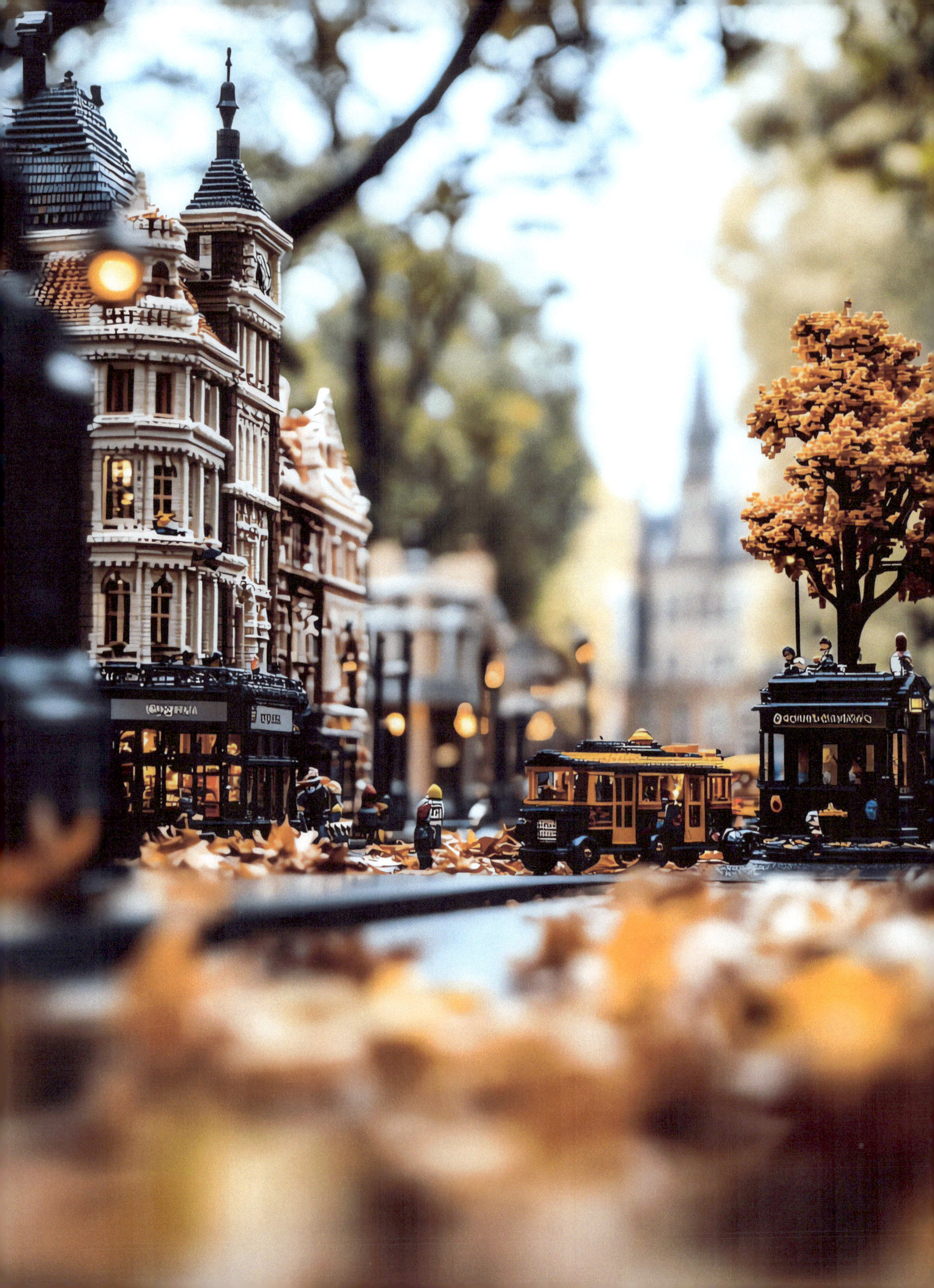

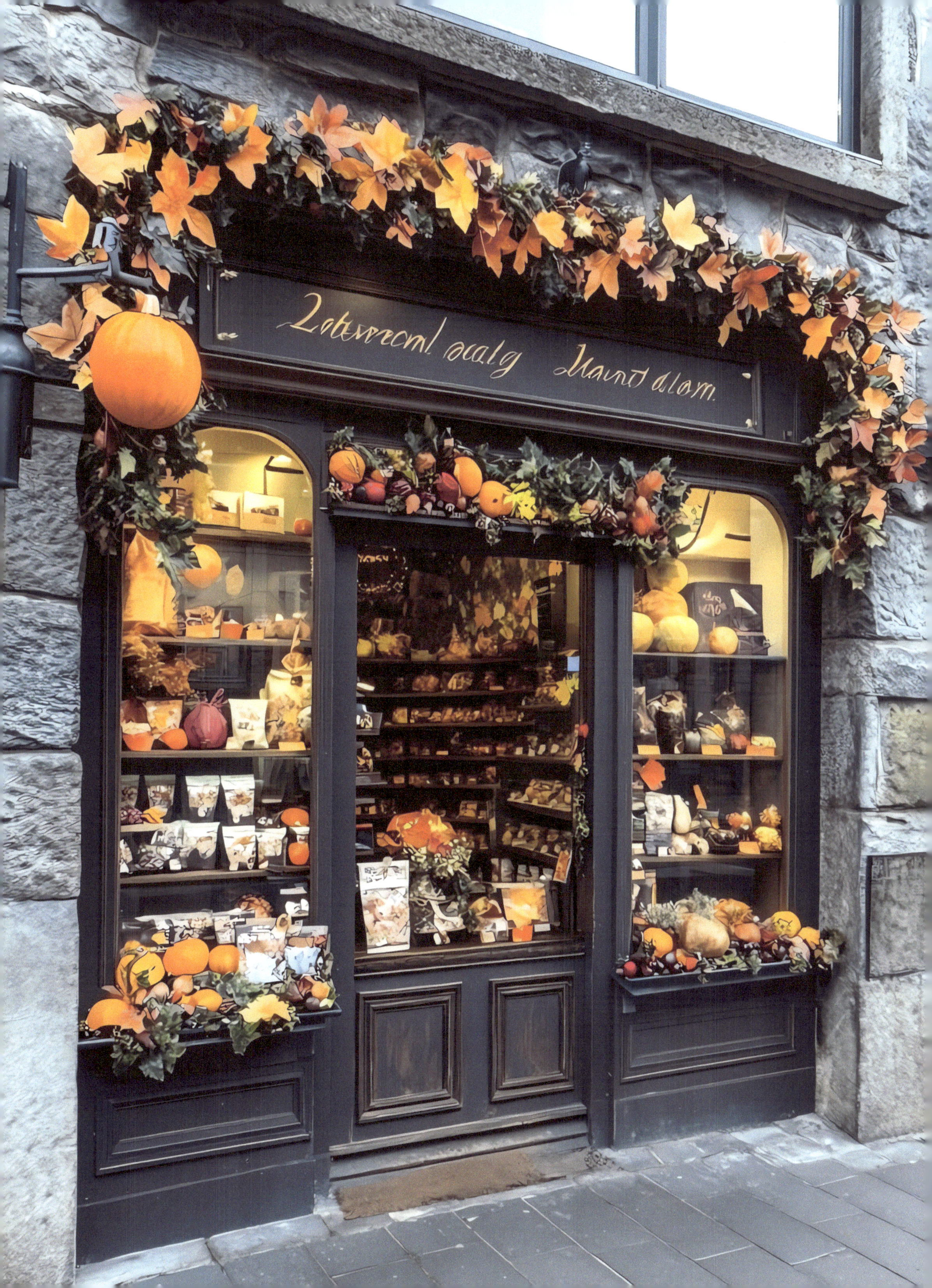

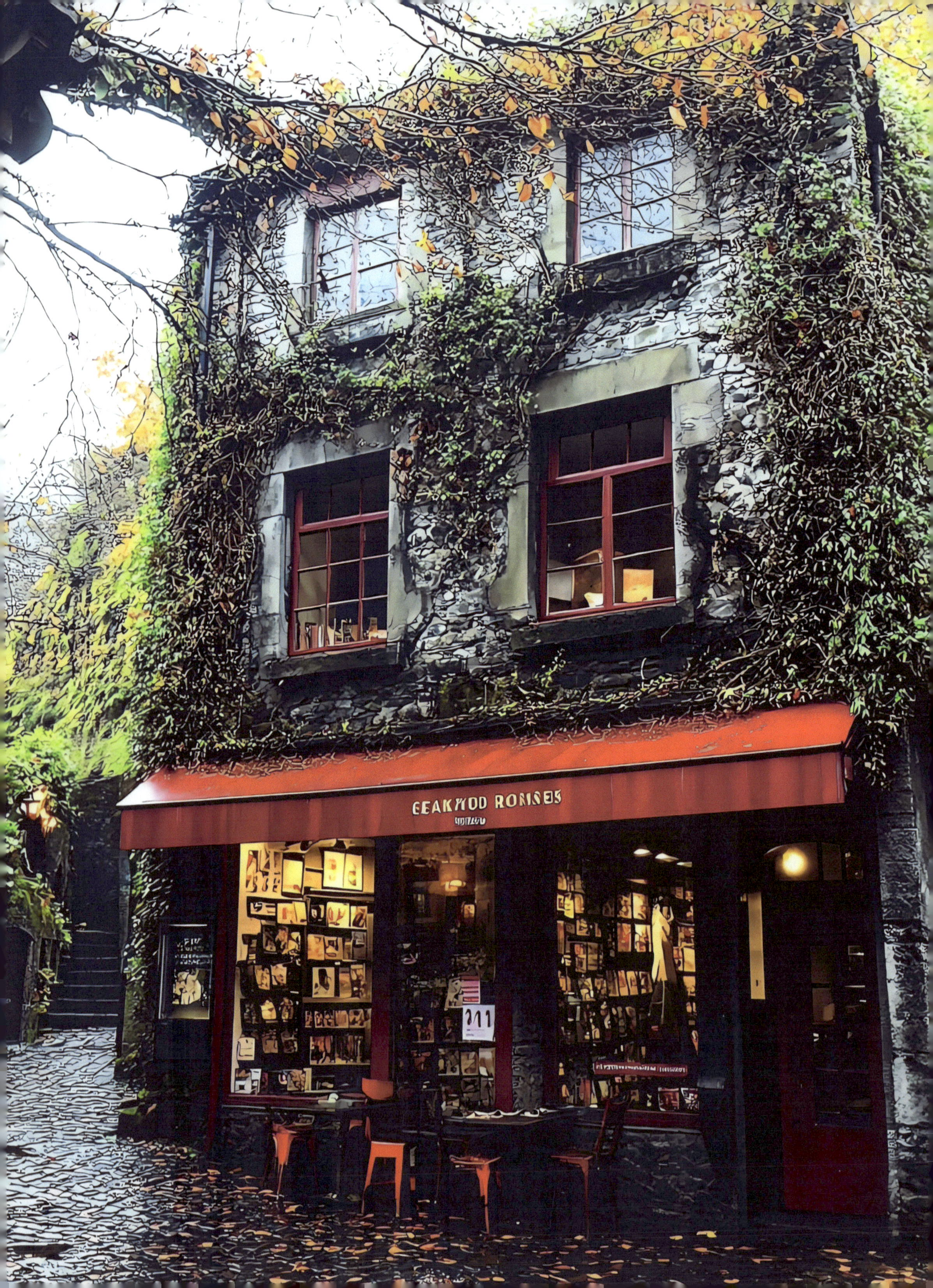

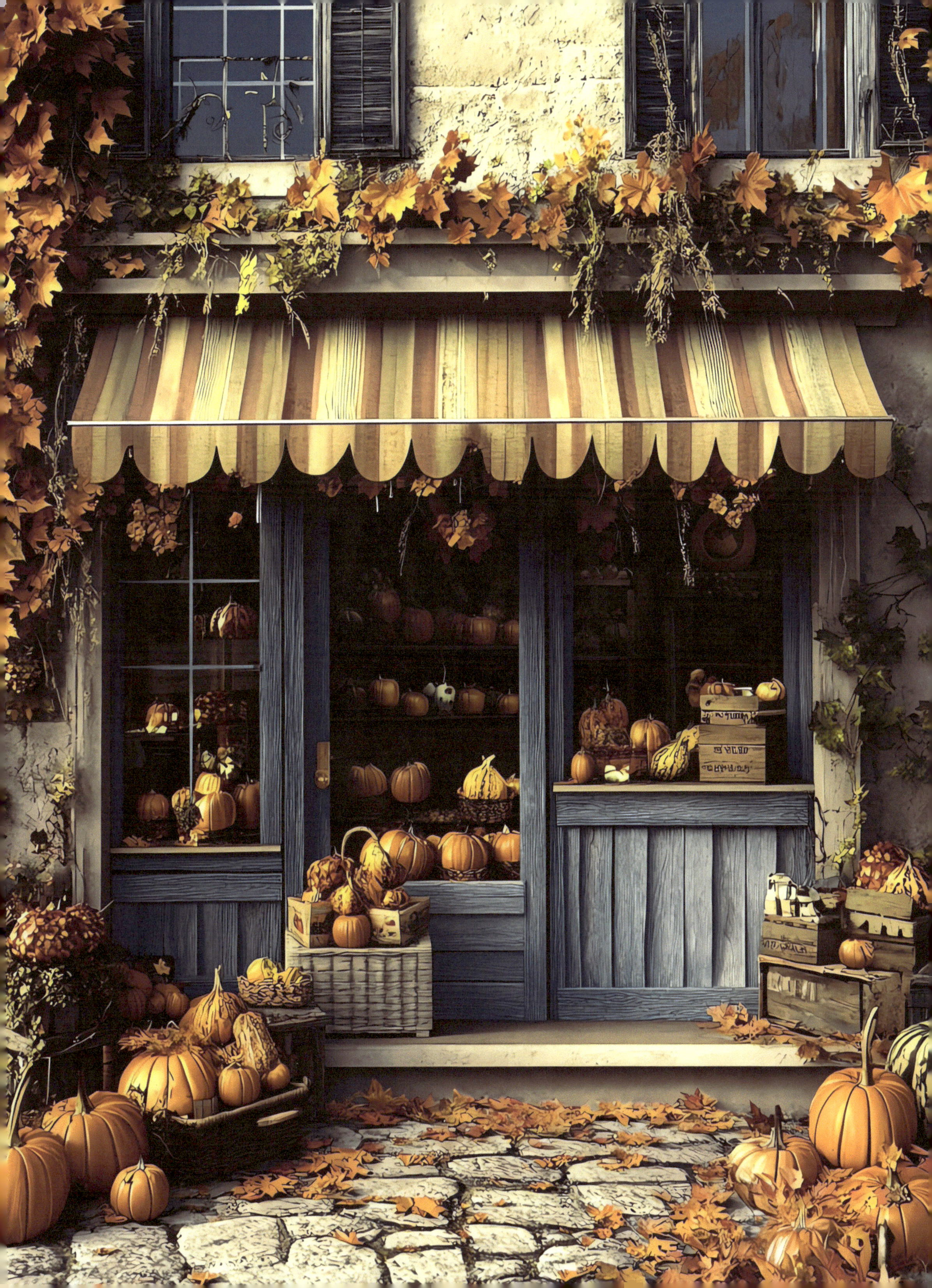

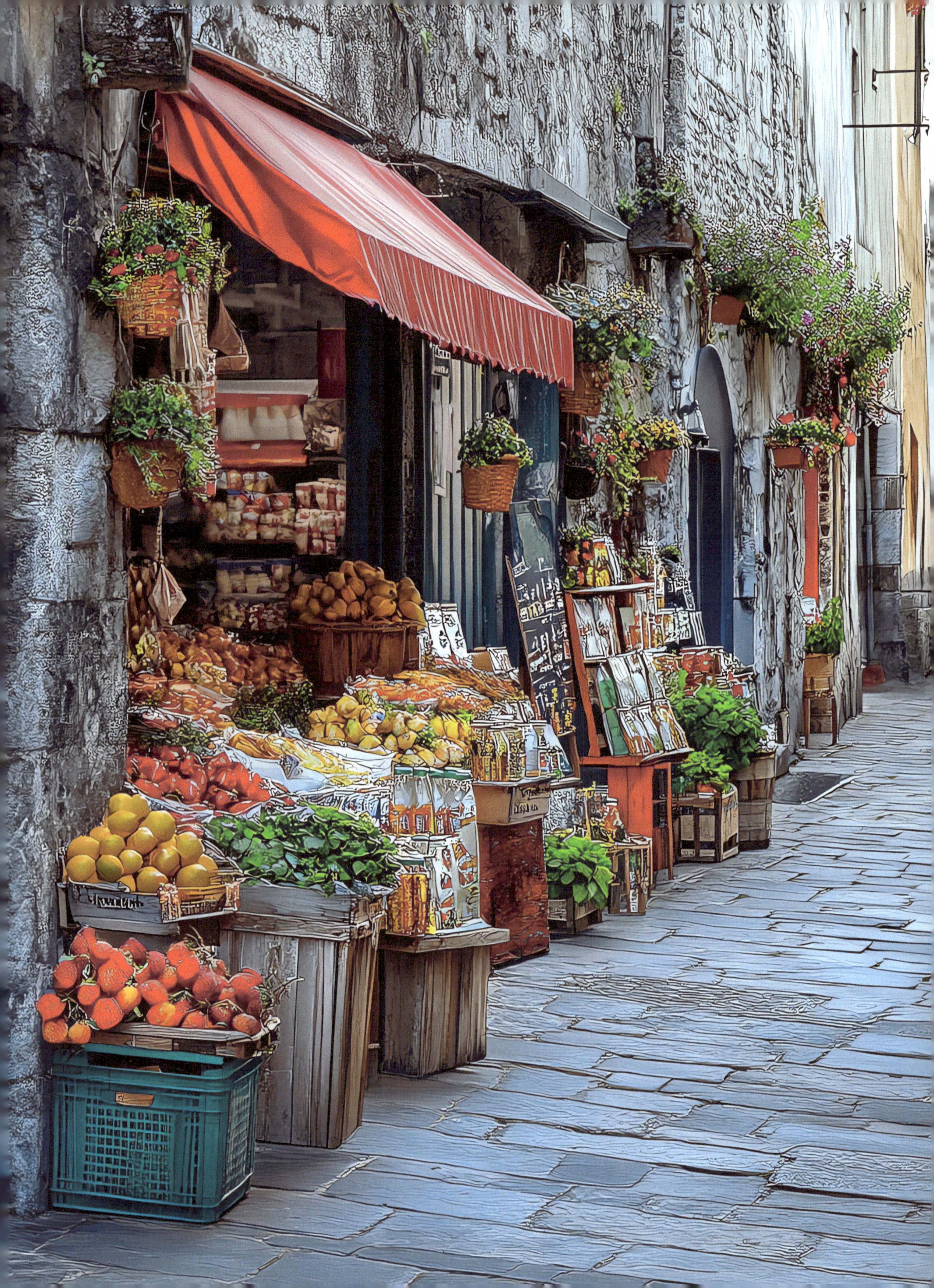

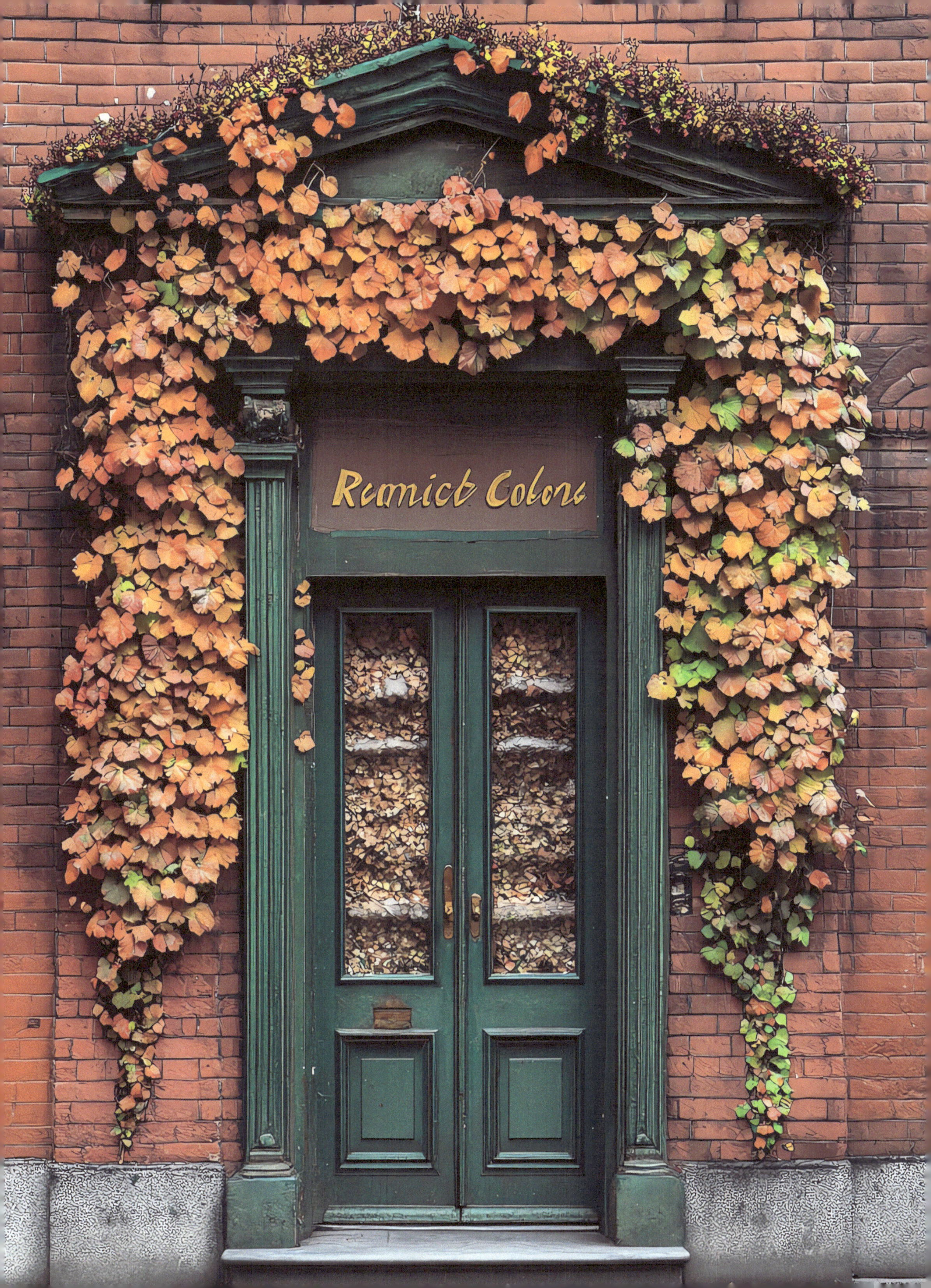
Remict Colors

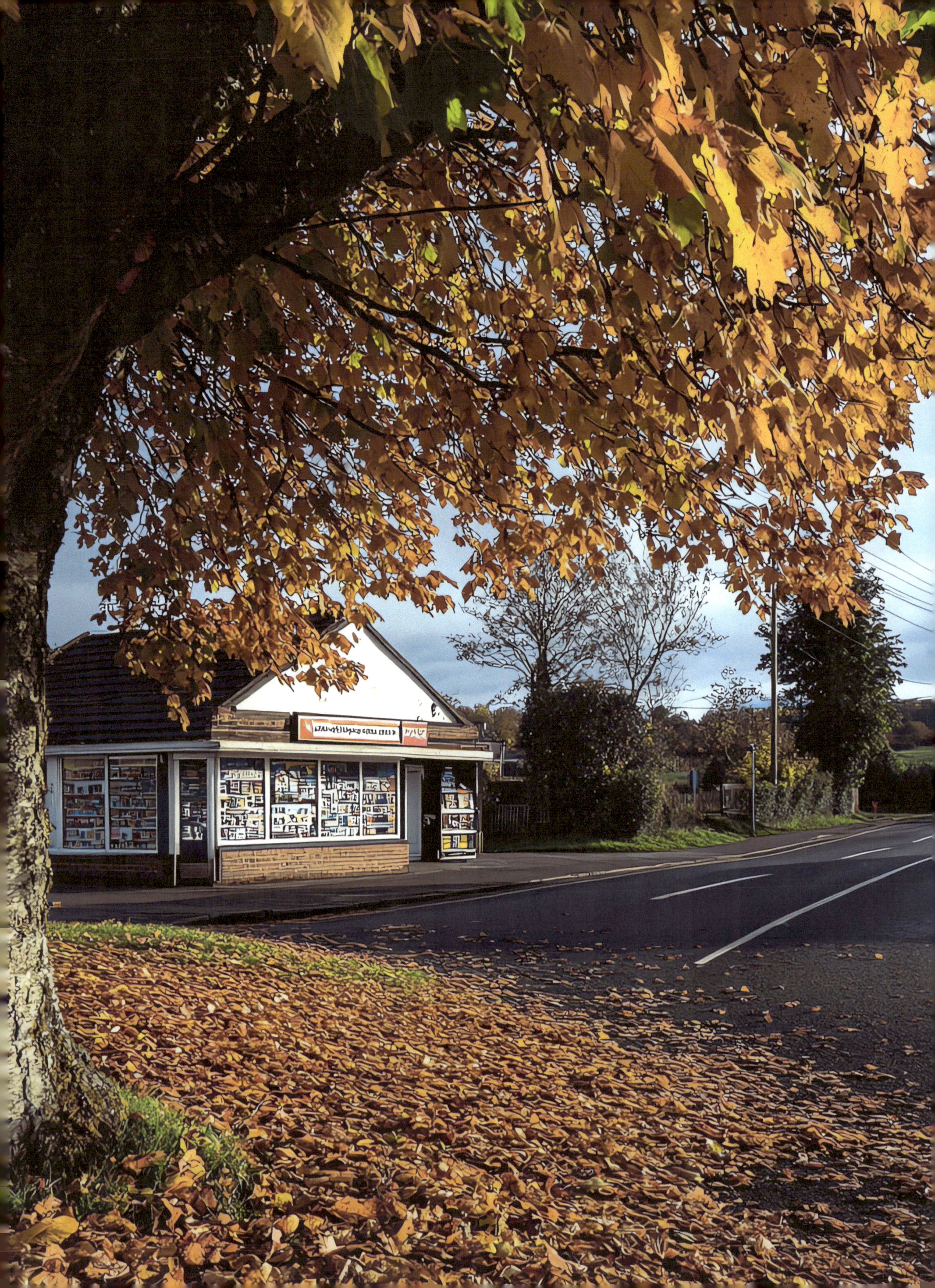

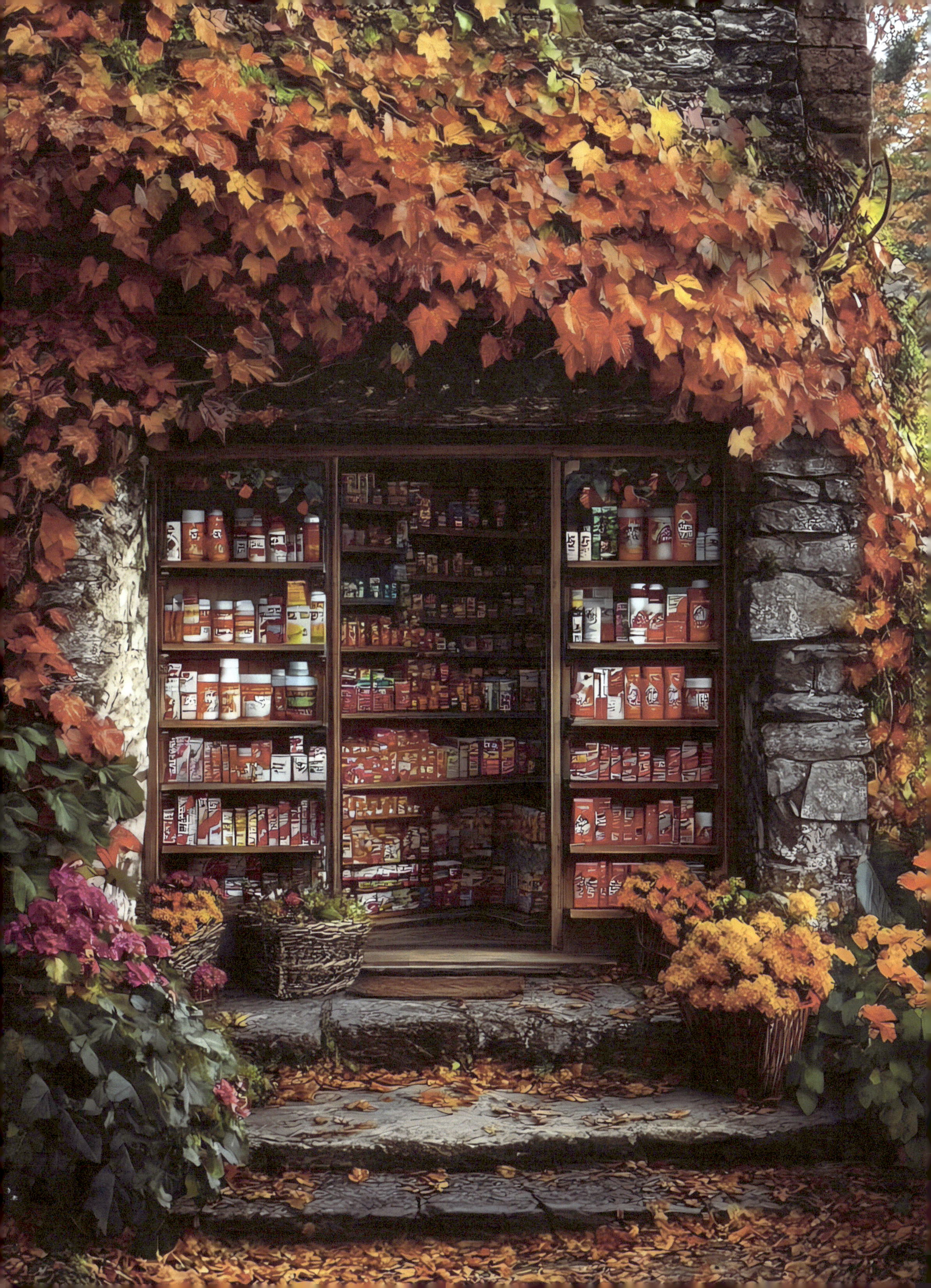

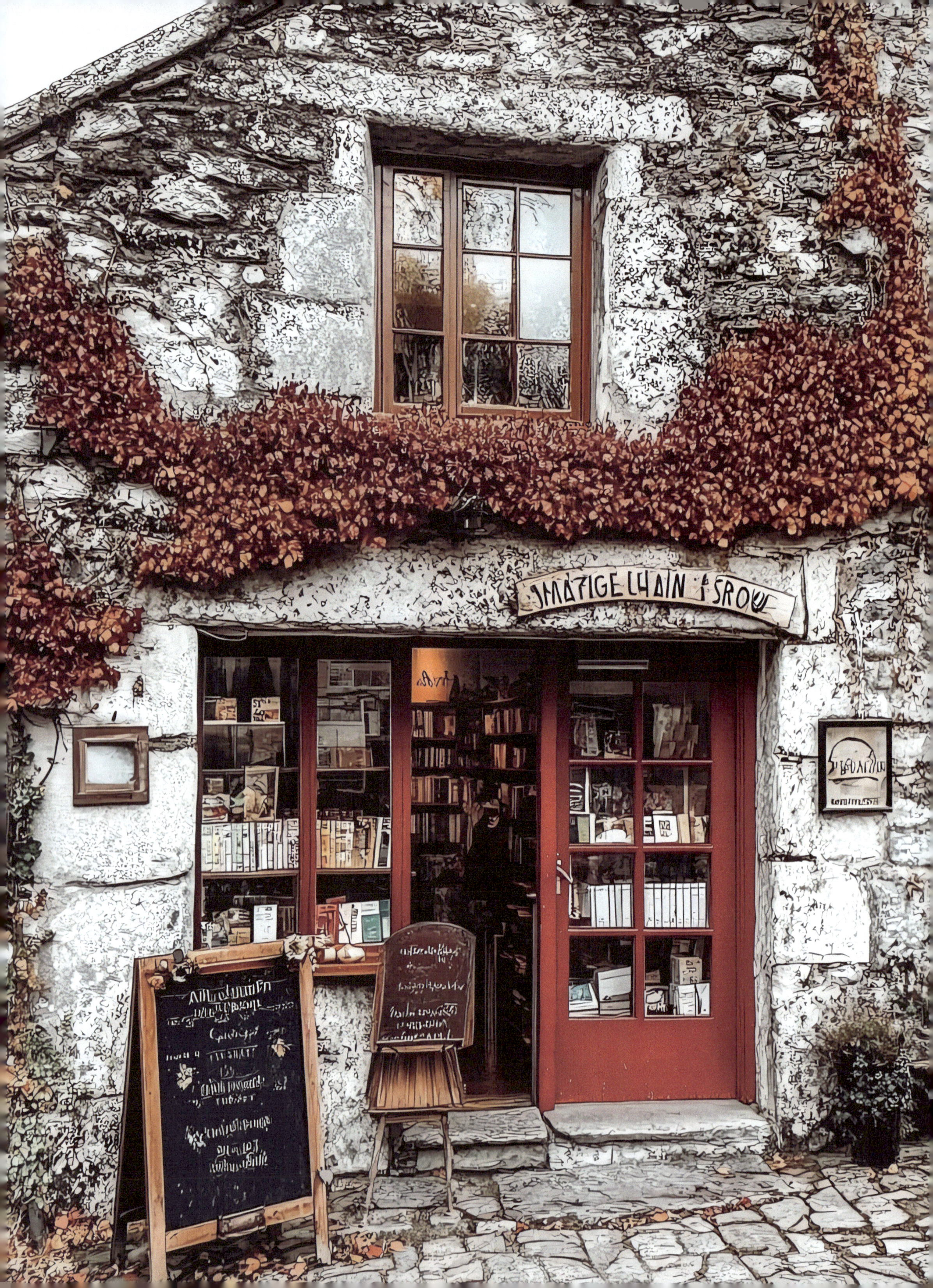

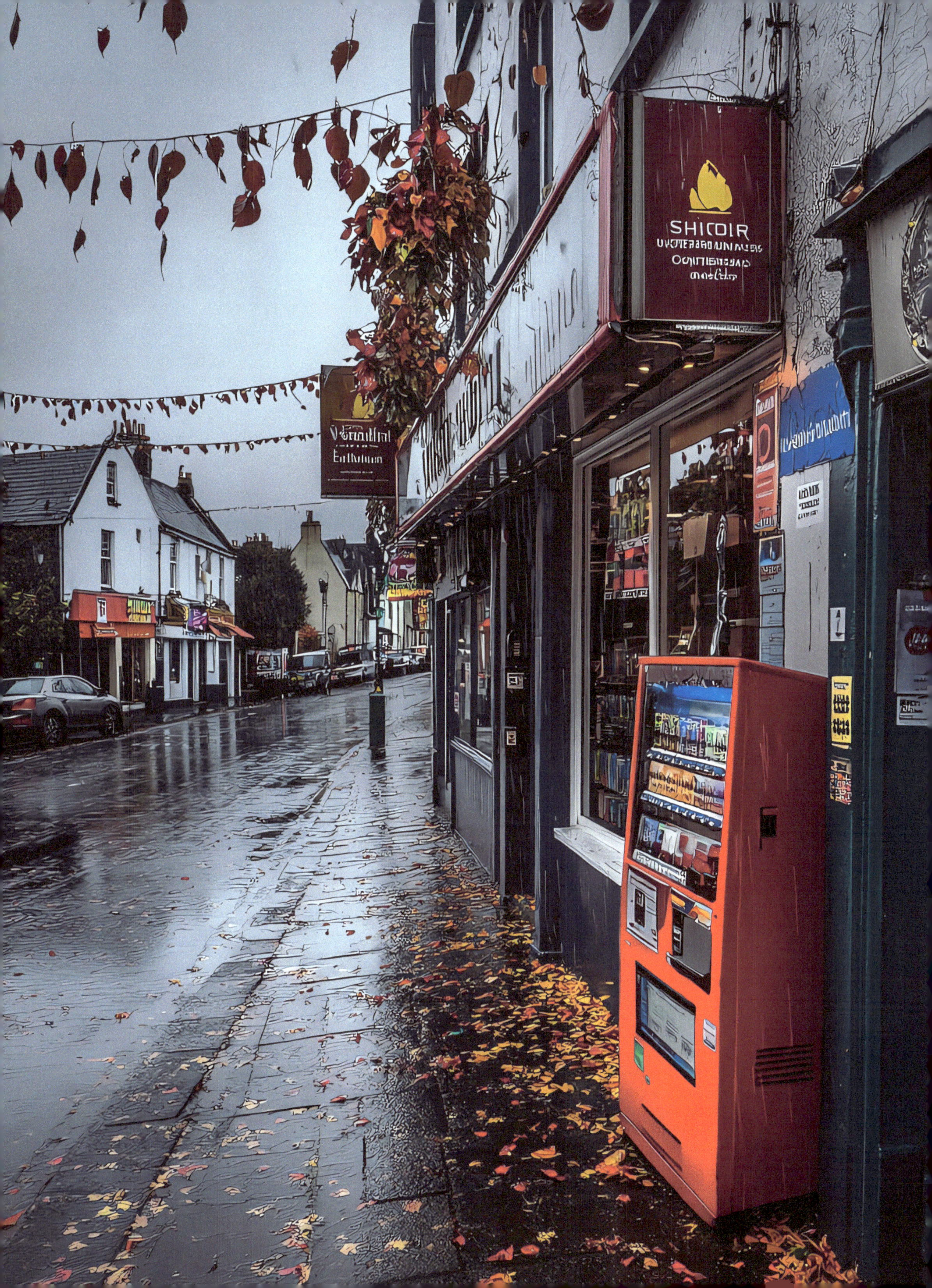
SHICOIR

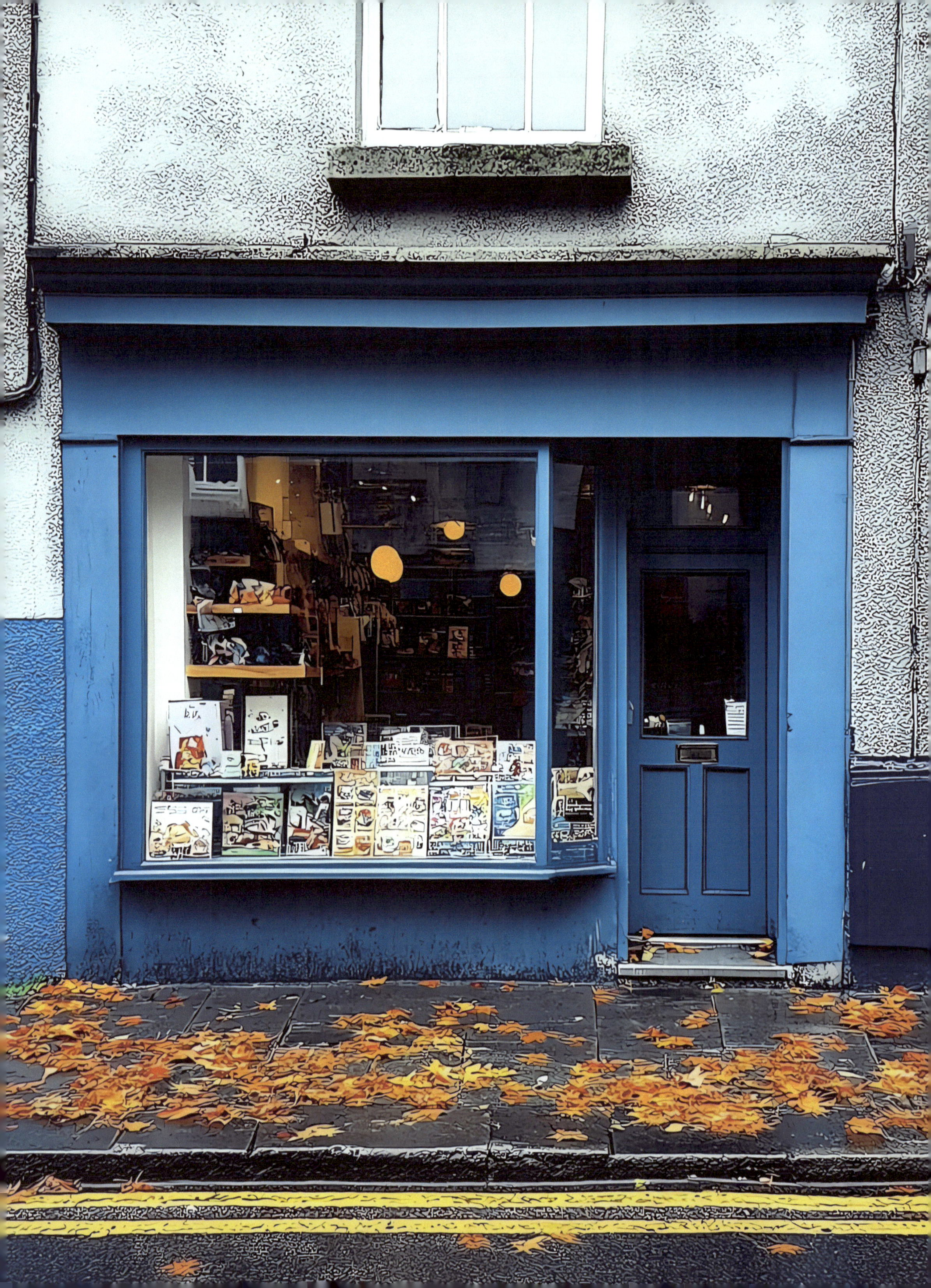

www.ingramcontent.com/pod-product-compliance
Lightning Source LLC
Chambersburg PA
CBHW040421220526
45473CB00004B/1319
* 9 7 9 8 3 0 3 3 4 4 6 4 8 *